PORTRAIT OF EPPING FOREST

Portrait of
EPPING FOREST

SIR WILLIAM ADDISON
(A Verderer)

ROBERT HALE · LONDON

© *Sir William Addison 1977*
First published in Great Britain 1977

ISBN 0 7091 6130 1

Robert Hale Limited
Clerkenwell House
Clerkenwell Green
London EC1R 0HT

PRINTED IN GREAT BRITAIN
BY LOWE & BRYDONE LTD, THETFORD, NORFOLK
PHOTOSET AND BOUND
BY WEATHERBY WOOLNOUGH,
WELLINGBOROUGH, NORTHANTS

CONTENTS

ILLUSTRATIONS

Between pages 128 and 129

MAP

The author thanks Mr Bernard Ward and Mr Alfred Qvist for help with illustrations, and is especially grateful to Miss Wendy Brimble for permission to reproduce ten of her late father's photographs.

PREFACE

EPPING FOREST is owned by the Corporation of London and administered in accordance with the terms of the Epping Forest Act 1878. For a hundred years the entire cost of management has been borne by 'City's Cash', a Corporation fund with an income derived mainly from estate rentals and the surplus from the running of the three great London markets. Not one penny piece has come out of rates or taxes.

This is a record of which the City is justly proud, and the approach of the Centenary of the passing of the 1878 Act seemed a fitting occasion for one who has served as a Verderer for twenty years, and studied the history of the Forest in detail for more than forty, to attempt belatedly to correct many false accounts of how it came to be saved from enclosure in the nineteenth century, and explain what really did happen.

It would be impossible to thank all who have been kind enough to check data and discuss both official records and personal memories with me. My greatest indebtedness is to Alfred Qvist, Superintendent of the Forest since 1949, and Bernard Ward, my brother Verderer since 1960. The principal City Officers have been kind enough to read the manuscript and offer valuable suggestions. The chairman of the Epping Forest Committee, Mr *Deputy* Sheppard, and the Deputy Chairman, Mr John T. Yates, have discussed various controversial matters with me, and I have been especially grateful to those two life-long friends of the Forest, Sir Stuart Mallinson and Sir Arthur Noble, for making their own notes available to me. These and other friends have saved me from many errors. For any that have escaped detection I am alone responsible.

Epping   WILLIAM ADDISON

"It gives me the greatest satisfaction to dedicate this beautiful Forest to the enjoyment of my people for ever."

Queen Victoria

CHAPTER I

KINGS TO COMMONERS

EPPING FOREST, an irregular crescent of heath and woodland straggling through the eastern suburbs of London from Forest Gate in the south to Thornwood in the north, is all that is left of the royal forest of Waltham, the favourite hunting ground of English sovereigns for six hundred years. The total area of Forest land is now slightly less than 6,000 acres, one-tenth of what it was when its bounds were fixed in a Perambulation of 1641. Two-thirds of this region is woodland, one-third rough grazing land and water. In length it is about twelve miles, and nowhere is it more than two miles wide.

It was never possible to determine the area of a royal forest precisely. Manwood in his *Treatise of the Forest Laws* (1598) defined such a tract as "a certain territory of woody grounds and fruitful pastures privileged for wild beasts and fowls of Forest chase and warren to rest and abide there in the safe protection of the King for his delight and pleasure". The boundary of such a territory was marked out by such natural features as streams, established highways, or large stones between which the deer could roam without let or hindrance.

The 1641 Perambulation fixed the River Lea from Bow Bridge to Roydon as the western boundary, the High Road from Bow to Havering as the southern boundary. The eastern boundary was defined by an irregular line running from the Romford road along the boundary of Havering Park to a point in the parish of Navestock, from which it continued along the River Roding to Abridge, and from there through Theydon Bois to enclose the parishes of Epping and Nazeing before reaching the Lea at Roydon. Within this region the River Roding formed a natural dividing line between the forests of Hainault and Epping, giving 17,000 acres to

Hainault and 43,000 to Epping. Most of the soil in Hainault Forest belonged to the Abbess of Barking, that in Epping Forest to the Abbot of Waltham, with these major exceptions: the manor of Chingford St Paul's belonged to the Dean and Chapter of St Paul's, the manors of Leyton Grange and West Ham to the Abbot of St Mary's Abbey, Stratford, and the manor of Cann Hall to the Prior of Holy Trinity, Westminster. At the Dissolution nearly the whole of the Waltham manors became Crown property; but they were regranted to lay landowners, whose successors in title were to complicate the issue when their enclosures were challenged in the nineteenth century.

Of these two great religious foundations, both Saxon in origin, which dominated the region throughout the Middle Ages, little remains to remind the visitor of their former power. Waltham still retains its noble church; Barking has only the Fire Bell Gate, a gate-tower with an upper chapel containing a decayed mid-twelfth-century rood with three figures, surviving from the proud foundation that William the Conqueror made his headquarters while the Tower of London was being built. Yet at the height of its fame Barking was the richest nunnery in England, with three queens in its roll of abbesses. And though proud to entertain kings, Barking did not neglect the poor. When King David of Scotland came south to visit his sister, Queen Maud, who was then Abbess, he found her washing the feet of lepers in the hospital founded for their care at Ilford.

Both the Abbess of Barking and the Abbot of Waltham were privileged to hunt hares and foxes in the Forest, and each year they received generous grants of venison from the royal hunters. Much of the income sustaining the abbeys was derived from sheep put out to graze on the marshes of the Thames Estuary and the Lea Valley. Their fuel came from the Forest, and as clearings were made in the woodland the abbots and abbesses built granges and established farms. So we may think of the Forest throughout the Middle Ages as a tract of waste and woodland with only two towns, the abbey towns of Barking and Waltham, but with a number of shooting lodges and small settlements sparsely dispersed across the rough pastures between them.

Waltham was the last of the abbeys to be dissolved by Henry VIII, and we may speculate on how different the town's history would have been if his original intention at the Dissolution had been fulfilled. A document has survived in the King's own handwriting expressing his intention to use part of the revenues of the abbeys to endow a number of bishoprics, and at the head of the list stands Waltham, designated as the cathedral city of Essex.

For more than a hundred years after the Dissolution Waltham continued in favour with Tudor and Stuart court favourites—whose names can still be seen in the parish registers. There were the Cecils (whose palace at Theobalds was exchanged for Hatfield), the Grevilles, the Dennys and many others of equal note. Perhaps the most spectacular occasion in Waltham's secular history was in 1603, when James I on his accession to the English throne was received by Robert Cecil and his neighbours with a brave display of loyalty, despite the fact that Cecil's father, Elizabeth's Burghley, had been chiefly responsible for the death of the new king's mother, Mary Queen of Scots, at Fotheringhay only a few years earlier. Stow tells us that Sir Edward Denny of Waltham rode out to meet the King, "attended on by a goodly company, in number seven-score, suitably apparelled in blue livery coats and white doublets, hats and feathers, and well mounted on horses with red saddles. Sir Edward, after humble duty done, presented his Majesty with a gallant horse, a rich saddle, and furniture correspondent being of great value". Thus at Waltham in 1603 was re-enacted the scene witnessed at Barking more than five hundred years earlier, when the Saxon thanes rode through the Forest to do homage to William the Conqueror.

It was under the Tudors and Stuarts that Waltham Forest, or Epping Forest as we now know it, reached its greatest fame as the favourite resort of kings and their courtiers. Visiting princes and ambassadors from their courts were entertained in the great houses that succeeded the abbeys as social centres—most lavishly at Copped Hall, Epping (then in Waltham parish), and at the old manor house at Wanstead.

Copped Hall had been a place of retirement for the abbots of Waltham. After remaining in the Crown for some time it was granted by Elizabeth I to Sir Thomas Heneage, Treasurer

of the Royal Chamber and Vice-Chamberlain of the Queen's
Household. Camden says of him that "for his elegancy of life
and pleasantness of speech" he was born for the court:
"Indeed he was about as perfect a man as had graced it—
learned and cultured, a lover of the muses and patron of their
followers". It was he who built the most magnificent of the
three Copped Halls that have occupied the site, and there he
continued the hospitality of the abbots to visiting potentates.
Elizabeth I was entertained in 1568. In 1595 there were
elaborate preparations for another visit, but they had to be
cancelled when smallpox broke out in the district. Among
other sovereigns entertained at Copped Hall were Charles II,
who dined with the Earl of Middlesex there in 1660, James II,
and William III, who dined and stayed the night on 4 April
1698 on his way to Newmarket. After Sir Thomas Heneage,
Copped Hall had a succession of distinguished owners including Lionel Cranfield, Earl of Middlesex, Lord Treasurer
and Master of the Court of Wards in James I's reign, and
Charles Sackville, the Earl of Dorset, who wrote the song:

> To all you ladies now at land
> We men at sea indite;
> But first would have you understand
> How hard it is to write.

He and his friends were the wildest set in England.

Wanstead is even richer in royal associations. Perhaps its
most colourful occasion was in 1553, when Mary Tudor, in
her progress to London to be crowned Queen, paused to
receive her sister, Elizabeth, attended by a thousand of the
most exalted among her subjects, amid scenes of such glory as
only a Tudor could evoke.

Other houses in the Forest came into favour at this time
and were either built or rebuilt. Birch Hall, Theydon Bois,
was the home of Sir Edward Elrington, an officer of the
Household to Edward VI, Mary and Elizabeth. A later house
of the same name is chiefly associated with the Buxton
family, and the estate is now the Forest Deer Sanctuary.
Gaynes Park was the home of Sir William FitzWilliam; Hill
Hall, Theydon Mount, the home of Sir Thomas Smith, whose
influence in Tudor politics is still inadequately appreciated.

With the Commonwealth all this splendour and gaiety vanished. The deer were the prey of poachers and the pageantry of the Royal Forest became no more than a memory. There was compensation in that the harsh Forest laws were no longer enforced; but anarchy ensued. Most of the red and fallow deer were killed off by desperate ex-soldiers of the Civil War who haunted the Forest and got their livelihood by selling venison in the London street markets. More seriously, the depredations of the poachers were matched by those of the local landowners who either engaged in or connived at the cutting of timber, which in point of fact was urgently needed in the middle of the seventeenth century while England was in competition with the Dutch for sea power. The Diary of Samuel Pepys gives a fair idea of what Epping Forest meant during the commercially competitive years that followed the restoration of Charles II to the throne. Courtiers like Sir Thomas Heneage of Epping, Sir William FitzWilliam of Theydon Garnon and the Earl of Leicester of Wanstead were succeeded by bankers and merchants, of whom the most redoubtable was Sir Josiah Child, whose son built the great house that was intended to be to the east of London what Hampton Court was to the west. His successors at Wanstead were to figure prominently later, and what is left of the grounds he laid out, and the avenues he planted, may still be seen. Wanstead Park is preserved with Epping Forest.

It is only by knowing something of the arrogant pride of these lords of the manors who succeeded the courtiers associated with the royal forest that we can understand the force of the storm that broke so unexpectedly on them in the nineteenth century. The large-scale cutting of trees that began in the seventeenth century continued into the eighteenth. Over 1,000 trees were felled and sold in 1721, over 2,000 in 1725, and it was estimated that in the ten years from 1713 to 1723 leave had been given to cut groves covering upwards of 680 acres. The rolls of the Court of Attachments for the years between 1713 and 1770 show that applications to cut specified groves were renewed at intervals as coppice wood from the trees felled earlier reached marketable growth. Connivance at these cuttings is shown in a statement made by Lord Rich that when he was Lieutenant of the Forest he never refused an application to cut or enclose the applicant's own woods. These applications disappear after 1710, either through laxity on the part of the officers of the court in recording them, or because trees were cut with impunity by owners of the soil. The laxity is understandable. It came to be regarded as sinful that all this potentially productive land should not be brought into cultivation. The Forest villages were expanding, and to those who moved in from other parts the restrictions imposed on all who lived within the confines of a royal forest made no sense at all. It is not surprising, therefore, that as Crown rights ceased to be exercised the Forest laws came to be regarded as irrelevant to the workaday life of the villages and fell into abeyance.

The deer, in particular, were regarded with disfavour. Arthur Young, the agriculturalist, writing in 1807, said:

> The adjacent Forests of Epping and Hainault are viewed as an intolerable nuisance, and are equally regarded as such at Chigwell and Loughton, where the farmers uniformly declare, that the privilege of commonage is by no means equal to the one-tenth part of the losses they constantly sustain from the deer in breaking down their fences, trespassing upon their fields, and destroying their crops either ripe or green. Against these depredators it is further alleged, that there are no fences, however laboriously contrived, expensive, and formidable against other animals, that will in any wise avail: add to this, that the evil is continually increasing, from the annual increase in the stock of deer.
>
> These Forests, so near the Metropolis are well known to be the nursery and resort of the most idle and profligate of men: here the undergraduates in iniquity commence their career with deer stealing, and here the more finished and hardened robber secretes himself from justice, or retires for a time with his plunder from his haunts in London, where his arrest is certain whenever it is determined by the master robber, or robber-catcher, that the actual robber is to be *done*.

It is clear that if everyone had agreed with the landowners and their tenant farmers, both the advantages and disadvantages of living in a region subject to the Forest laws would have disappeared together. Others, as we shall discover, had a different view of the privilege of commonage, although we may doubt whether they appreciated how they came to have it. Stated briefly, the Crown enjoyed the right to hunt over all cultivated land within the Forest, which was not much fun for the farmers, who were free to grow their crops in the normal manner, but were not permitted to erect fences of a height that would keep out a doe with her fawn. It is from this restriction that we get the name 'Lippitt' in Lippitts Hill, a name derived from 'leaphatch'—a low gate in a fence that could be leaped by deer.

The times for hunting fixed by the Forest laws were: the hart and the buck from the Feast of St John the Baptist (23 June) to Holyrood Day (25 September), the hind and the doe from Holyrood Day to Candlemas (14 February), the fox from Christmas Day to Candlemas. These were strictly enforced by the Forest courts, whose prime purposes were the protection of the Crown rights to vert and venison and the control of enclosures. Vert, for the purpose of the Act, included any form of herbage required by the deer, venison any beast of chase including the hare. When fully exercised, the restrictions imposed by the Forest laws were severe. The penalties could be savage. It was originally as compensation for these restrictions that commoning was permitted. It is doubtful whether it can always have been a right in law. Even as regards walking on a common, it has been held that the law is that no one has a right to go on to a common, but equally no one has a right to turn anyone off! But whatever the law in general may have been, long-established custom appears to have given special privileges to those who enjoyed commonage in Epping Forest. The most important of these was the privilege enjoyed by owners and occupiers of land within its bounds to depasture their cattle over its entire area, a privilege that could be claimed as a prescriptive right because it predated the division of the area into manors. Any rights established later were subject to it. There was, however, a restriction, and this was to prove decisive later. The right of commonage was not enjoyed during the fence month of fifteen days before and fifteen days after old Midsummer Day (6 July) when the does and their fawns required undisturbed quiet. This meant that anyone who wanted to run out cattle

must have land of his own to accommodate them during the
time of prohibition. As we shall see, the fact that this had not
been taken into the reckoning when the Forest courts ceased
to function was to provide considerable ground for dispute.

Along with the right of pasturage for cattle went the right
of pannage for pigs while there was mast on the ground, that
is to say, from fifteen days before Michaelmas to forty days
after. Sheep were excluded at all times.

The persons appointed to administer the Forest laws enjoyed privileges of status that they were as reluctant to
relinquish as the commoners were to relinquish commoning.
The principal officer of the Forest was the Steward, afterwards called the Lord Warden, an hereditary office held for
centuries by the de Vere Earls of Oxford. It was an office of
great dignity; but some of the rights and privileges of the
holder came into question when illegal enclosures, either
made or sanctioned by the Earls Tylney and Viscounts
Wellesley as Lord Wardens, came to be challenged in the
courts in the nineteenth century. Immediately below the Lord
Warden came the Lieutenant of the Forest, who was supported by a number of Master Keepers, who were themselves
men of lord-of-the-manor status, and were assisted by under-
keepers, regarders, woodwards and reeves in carrying out
their practical duties. The Lord Warden also had power to
appoint a Deputy Warden, a Riding Forester and a Purlieu-
Ranger, to watch over the interests of the Crown along the
borders of the Forest.

The duties of the other officers can be deduced from their
titles. The foresters' duties were to supervise the game and
beasts of chase, in particular to see that the deer were not
disturbed during the fence month. It was their duty to ex-
peditate dogs—cut three claws off the fore feet of all dogs in
the Forest to prevent them chasing the deer.

The only one of these practical offices continued today in
its original form is that of reeve. These are still nominated by
parish vestries and are required to mark all commonable
beasts with parish marks, which take the form of a letter of
the alphabet surmounted by a crown. Originally, when called
agisters, they had the additional duty of assisting in driving
the Forest to prevent improper commoning. These were the

administrative officers. The judicial officers were the Verderers, who presided over the Forest court of Attachments—the forty-day court—or Woodmote, which was the oldest court in the country with the single exception of the coroner's court. They presided also at Swainmote, where more serious offenders were tried by a jury of freeholders of the Forest summoned three times a year. The most serious offences of all were tried by visiting judges at the court of the Chief Justice in Eyre, commonly called the Justice Seat. The Verderers were four in number and held office for life. Manwood describes them as judicial officers of the King's Forest, "sworn to maintain and keep the assizes of the Forest, and also to view, receive, and enroll the attachments and presentments of all manner of trespasses of the Forest, of vert and venison". Their title is French, but their office is claimed by some authorities to have been instituted before the Norman Conquest by Canute, and to have provided that:

> There shall henceforth be four of the best freemen, who have their accustomed wages secure, constituted in every province of the kingdom to distribute justice, together with due punishments as to the matters of the Forest, to all my people, as well English as Danish, throughout the whole kingdom of England, which four we think fit to be called the Chief Men of the Forest.

The method of appointment appears to have varied. In some forests they were appointed by the Crown, in others—and Waltham was one—they were elected by the freeholders.

Although the Verderers presided at Swainmote they did not sentence. Convicted offenders were committed from this court for sentence, usually on bail, to Justice Seat, which seldom seems to have sat more than once in three years. These triennial visits by the Chief Justice in Eyre must have been events attended by fear and trepidation. There were two Chief Justices in Eyre, one for the forests north of Trent, the other for forests south. They were always peers, and it was their duty not only to sentence offenders but also to conduct general enquiries into the affairs of the forest, for which, as well as for trials, a jury of freeholders, varying in number from eighteen to twenty-four, was impanelled. The jurors were rewarded for their services with venison, the Verderers with free deer.

The perquisites of office appear to have been considerable. We often say that we are proud of our tradition of unpaid voluntary work in England, much of which stems from the traditions of the lay magistracy—the Great Unpaid. In fact, most offices of the Crown until modern times carried profit of one kind or another. The Lord Warden of Waltham Forest was also Keeper of the Royal Park and Mansion at Havering-atte-Bower, and had a salary as well as various perquisites, including "all waifs and strays", whatever that may have meant, all fines imposed by Swainmote, the second best oak tree in every wood, one bow, one broad arrow, and one penny in the shilling from all wood sold. Moreover then as now,

> Big fleas had little fleas,
>   Upon their backs to bite 'em,
> And little fleas had lesser fleas,
>   And so *ad infinitum.*

In 1774, Mr Heathcote, whose descendants have been lords of the manor of Chingford Earls down to our own day, paid Earl Tylney, who was then Lord Warden, £550 for the grant of the office of Master Keeper of the Chingford Walk to himself, his wife, his son, and so forth. It was a good investment. A Master Keeper had by law grants of venison, timber and certain fees. At the time when Mr Heathcote paid his money these fees were calculated at £36 10s. Alderman Copeland, Master Keeper of the Walthamstow Walk in the nineteenth century, in giving evidence to the Select Committee on Royal Forests in 1863, stated that Master Keepers had the privilege of shooting in the Forest and the appointing of an under-keeper, who was paid by the Crown. They were entitled to one buck annually, but the Master Keeper of the Walthamstow Walk had only claimed this once. It was an occasion he well remembered, because when his under-keeper shot it he got into trouble. It turned out that this particular buck was being kept on clover for one of the Verderers!

The Master Keeper's symbol of office was a horn, which he was required to present on his knees at the Justice Seat after the Lieutenant had presented his baton. The office of Verderer, although carrying fewer perquisites, was in great demand among local landowners during the eighteenth century. The cost of being elected was usually £500 or £600; but on one famous occasion (in 1798) competition was so keen between Col. Burgoyne of Mark Hall, Harlow, and Mr Bosanquet of Leytonstone, that the poll was kept open for fourteen days and people were brought from all over the country to vote. The cost to Mr Bosanquet was £7,000, to Col. Burgoyne (who was elected) £10,000. The privileges of office were not sufficient to compensate for that kind of expenditure, although the sittings of the courts were not uncongenial. On 3 June 1723, for example, it was ordered that those who were granted licences to shoot, hunt, etc. in the Forest should not take them up until they had paid to the court three dozen of wine. The principal attraction of the office was undoubtedly the local status it conferred on the holder. At the height of their power, nobody living in a Forest parish could take a lodger into his house without the permission of a Verderer.

The Verderer's Oath, as taken on appointment by Col. Palmer in 1842, was:

I will truly serve our Sovereign Lady the Queen in the office of Verderer in the Forest of Waltham. I will, to the utmost of my power and knowledge, do for the profit of the Queen, as far as it doth appertain to my duty. I will preserve and maintain the ancient rights and franchises of Her Crown. I will not conceal from Her Majesty any rights or privileges, or any offence, either in vert or venison, or any other thing. I will not withdraw or abridge any default, but will endeavour myself to manifest and redress the same, and if I cannot do it of myself, I will give knowledge thereof unto the Queen, or unto her Justice of the Forests. I will deal indifferently with all the Queen's liege people. I will execute the laws of the Forest, and do equal justice, as well unto the poor as unto the rich, in that which appertaineth to mine office. I will not oppress any person under colour thereof, for any reward, favour, or malice. All these things I will keep to the utmost of my power, and observe justice. So help me God.

George Palmer stated, in giving evidence before the Select Committee on Royal Forests in 1863, that it had been the custom for the Verderers to appoint a clerk of the court. The Lord Warden appointed a steward, who by custom was a professional gentleman, and the Verderers had generally nominated the same person to be their clerk. His records of the courts were kept at the Lord Warden's house.

All this was pleasant enough; but too anachronistic to survive when it interfered with the inevitable inroads of urbanization, and those who enjoyed privileges as officers of the Forest strongly resented equally well-established privileges when exercised by commoners. Landowners enjoyed being Verderers; they resented not being allowed to enclose the land in their own manors. Those who were not Verderers resented being told that they could not so much as fell trees on their own land without permission from the Verderers because vert included all trees and underwood, while fruit-bearing trees such as crab, hawthorn, blackthorn, whitethorn and holly were classed as special vert. Even as late as the nineteenth century, Forest officers exercised their right to enter enclosed woods in the Forest to cut 'browst' for winter food for the deer, and the cutting of fruit-bearing trees was punishable by confiscation of the horse and cart that carried it, in addition to the fine imposed by the Verderers for cutting common vert.

The speed of change was accelerated by the rapid growth of London in the eighteenth century. Already in 1722, Defoe in his *Tour of the Eastern Counties* had noticed that all the towns and villages he passed through after crossing Bow Bridge had greatly increased in size during the last twenty or thirty years. Stratford, he thought, must have doubled its population. Similar growth was to be seen at Leyton, Walthamstow, Woodford and Wanstead. He noticed the increase in large and handsome houses, occupied either by wealthy London citizens who could afford two houses, one in the City and one in the country, or by retired merchants. He was witnessing the transformation of the Forest into a pleasant rural area associated not with the Court but with the City. Similar development was to be seen all round London; but here, Defoe noted, there was a marked air of respectability. It must have been an unexpected characteristic, having regard to the racy traditions of the region; but he was perfectly right. The region was coming under the influence of bankers and merchants of a very different kind from Sir Josiah Child. Many of them came from East Anglia, which had a strong moral tradition. In the following century, the characteristic of respectability became even more marked under the influence of the great Quaker families: Frys, Gurneys, Barclays, and their kinsfolk the Buxtons, who always denied being Quakers, but had as much Quaker blood in their veins as any of them. They were all people of high integrity, with a lofty conception of public service and social consciences well in advance of their times. Most had large families. To take one example, when the widow of Sir Thomas Fowell Buxton, one of the first Verderers appointed under the 1878 Act, died in 1911 at the age of ninety-seven, she left 120 descendants. She herself was born a Gurney, and we may take it that every one of those descendants became a person of influence.

They were all open-air families. Dignified as many of them were in later life, they could still be seen leading their children through the Forest each morning on strings of ponies before changing into City clothes to be driven up to London. They also had a curious rebel streak in them, and it was this that made Sir Fowell Buxton and his brother, Edward North Buxton, such fitting champions when the time came to salvage from the wreckage of this ancient royal forest the rights of the commoners, and in the name of the commoners to recreate these thousands of acres of waste and woodland for the benefit of the public as an open space preserved, not for the sport of princes or the relaxation of City merchants, but for the pleasure and recreation of the People.

CHAPTER II

ILLEGAL ENCLOSURES

THE FAILURE of the Forest courts to act against illegal enclosures was already being criticized in the 1840s. The *Essex
Standard* for 14 July 1843 had an account of a meeting of
freeholders, copyholders, and other residents in the Forest
parishes which had been held at the White Hart, Woodford,
to receive the report of a special committee that had been
appointed on 5 December 1842 to examine complaints about
the illegal enclosure of forest land. It had been an angry
meeting, vigorously protesting against illegal enclosures and
encroachments and demanding that they be stopped.

In demanding immediate action in 1843 it is unlikely that
anyone saw the problem as other than parochial. Epping
Forest was held to be common land, which the protesters
probably thought meant public property. They could not be
blamed for thinking so, because at that time little was known
about the rights of commoners or the legal control of
common land. They would certainly not feel required, as we
do today, to consider commoners' rights in Epping Forest in
relation to commoners' rights over more than a million acres
of common land in England as a whole, together with more
than four hundred and fifty thousand acres in Wales. It is
surprising how few of those who wrote and spoke about
commoners' rights in those days appear to have understood
that since Norman times most common land has been private
property: that the term 'common land' does not mean land
with common ownership, but land that is held subject to
certain privileges of use by the commoners. In most commons
the soil and what lies in it belongs to the lord of the manor
and carries all the safeguards that apply to other forms of
landed property. Despite this, however, rights of use are as

strong as rights of ownership. Their strength is in their anti-
quity and in the fact that the rights of all the commoners are
the rights of each individual one of them, which means that a
single commoner can veto any change in these rights even if
the majority are in favour of it. Rights of common date from
the time when fields were cultivated in common and the
surrounding waste was free for all as grazing land. If these
rights had been conferred by a benevolent landowner the
question of withdrawal or variation might be comparatively
simple. The basic fact about commoners' rights is that they
were already in existence in Norman times when manorial
rights were conferred on the lords and when the laws govern-
ing private property were formulated. But for this it is unlikely that any of the large areas of common land found near
populous towns and cities would have been preserved. The
historian Maitland, in *Township and Borough,* tells us about
the fight put up by the burgesses of Cambridge against the
Norman sheriff Picot, who, they contended, had reduced
their common pasture by building a mill on it. Only the
strength of ancient rights could have preserved from enclosure
the thousand-acre Town Moor at Newcastle-upon-Tyne, the
240-acre Saxon common at Southampton, and more than
2,600 acres within the bounds of the old London County
Council. Some of these rights of common were in respect of
land in parishes remote from those to which they were
attached. In Essex, many inland parishes had rights to pasture
on the marshes. Waltham Abbey and Walthamstow were
two Forest parishes enjoying such rights. The most notable of
those surviving is found at Wallasea Island, which is still
divided among the five mainland parishes of Canewdon,
Paglesham, Eastwood, Great Stambridge and Little Wakering,
with ditches defining their respective commons. In Epping
Forest, by contrast, the commoners in all the parishes enjoy
rights of pasturage throughout the Forest area. No ditches
divide it.

In most commons the most jealously guarded rights have
been those of pasturage and the gatherings of wood for winter
fuel. It was the threat to these that so enraged the meeting at
Woodford in 1843. It was also pointed out that gravel and
sand had been removed with impunity for years; but the chief

ground of complaint was that enclosures had now reached proportions that put the parishioners' rights of lopping and pasturage in peril.

In circumstances so complex, the Epping Forest residents assembled at Woodford were fortunate in having at their meeting a lawyer named Watts, who lived in Theydon Bois and had taken the trouble to acquaint himself both with the position in Epping Forest and with that in other royal forests similarly threatened. There was no doubt in his mind as to who should be required to act: it was the Verderers, who, he explained, were either appointed by the Crown or elected by the freeholders to maintain the Sovereign's rights under the Forest laws. Equally under those laws, they were charged with the duty to do justice between common man and common man in respect of the Forest laws and the Crown rights, and among those rights were the rights of pasturage and lopping. Mr Watts advised his audience, no doubt correctly, that whatever might be the position with regard to the Crown rights in Epping Forest, the commoners' rights remained, and it was the duty of the Verderers to guard them. They still had, he contended, power to stop illegal enclosures, and he urged that if no other way could be found to compel the Verderers to act, a petition should be presented to Parliament. He added that in fairness to the Verderers it was only right to inform the meeting that they had, he believed, considered the question and failed to reach agreement on a proper course of action. The Court of Attachments, at which applications to enclose were dealt with, had not functioned for the past seventeen years. It would not be difficult to convene such a court; but the Verderers doubted whether they still possessed the powers they were supposed to have. They were in still greater doubt as to how effective those powers would prove to be if they did exercise them. There would be no point in imposing penalties they were incapable of enforcing. Such action would only bring them into ridicule. But in spite of those doubts, two of the Verderers, William Whitaker Maitland of Loughton and George Palmer of Nazeing, were in favour of putting their authority to the test. The other two, Henry John Conyers and John Lockwood, pointed out that most of the forest courts in England had fallen into abeyance and expressed the fear that any attempt to revive them might only lead to the abolition of the office of Verderer and put an end to any good they might do.

At this point in the meeting Mr Davies of High Beach got up and pointed out that the Verderers of Epping Forest were elected by the freeholders and it was, therefore, for the freeholders to call a meeting "to compel them to do justice, as they are called on to do by the Queen and the Sheriff, in open court". This all seemed straightforward enough, and as Mr Davies came from the northern part of the Forest there would probably have been no difficulty about calling such a meeting. William Whitaker Maitland and George Palmer, two of the Verderers living in the northern parishes, would have welcomed one and popular opinion would almost certainly have supported them, although it may be doubted whether it would have supported Henry John Conyers as a person, for reasons that will be mentioned later. But popular opinion might have been very different in the southern parishes, where building pressure was already a threat as London expanded into Essex.

No one in 1843 would be able to estimate accurately the effect of two new factors in local government, namely, the recent arrival in Essex of major industries that were rapidly to displace agriculture in the south-west corner of the county, and the opening in 1840 of a station of the Eastern Counties Railway at Lea Bridge. From the 'forties onwards the urbanization of the old Forest villages gained momentum rapidly, and as the population increased, the proper supervision of so large an area of waste land in and around the villages became a serious problem. In a utilitarian age it was regarded as intolerable that these thousands of acres of good land should not be brought into use. Parliament itself not only connived at the enclosing of land in the nineteenth century, it actually encouraged it. In 1848 a Parliamentary Committee recommended that Hainault Forest should be disafforested and that the Crown should sell its forestal rights in Epping Forest to the lords of its nineteen manors, two of whom were the Verderers, Henry John Conyers and William Whitaker Maitland. It is obvious that this recommendation must have

placed these two Verderers in a dilemma. As loyal subjects of
the Crown and officers of a royal forest they had one duty, as
custodians of the Forest rights for the benefit of the freeholders and commoners they had another. These two duties
were not necessarily in conflict; but both were in conflict
with their private interests as landowners and their sense of
the inevitability of change.

The first trial of strength came in 1851. In that year the
son of the man who had dissipated the Wanstead inheritance
and brought ruin on the Tylneys recovered the Wanstead
Park estate from his father's mortgagees and took legal advice
on ways and means he might employ to put himself into a
strong financial position. On receiving this advice his first
move was to instruct Isaac Lake, the tenant of Aldersbrook
Farm, to enclose and bring into cultivation thirty-four acres of
waste at Wanstead Flats. This so angered the well-to-do local
merchants and bankers that Sir Thomas Fowell Buxton,
Richard Plaxton of Cann Hall and Alderman Copeland of
Walthamstow invited many of their influential neighbours to
meet them at the London Tavern, Fenchurch Street, on 28
April 1852, with a view to seeking legal advice on what the
rights of the new owner of Wanstead were, bearing in mind
that he might well claim to be the hereditary holder of the
ancient title of Lord Warden of the Forest and all the
privileges attached to that office. When challenged, he did
claim the office in his mother's right and exercised its prerog-
atives. At the final settlement the office was abolished and the
trustees of Lord Mornington were awarded £300 for loss of
their hereditary rights (see page 43). Feeling at the meeting
was high in protest against the enclosure, and it was resolved
to take counsel's opinion on its legality. If this proved favourable to the opposers it was further resolved to test the legality
in the courts by persuading a local freeholder to break down
the enclosing fence and drive in his cattle. Richard Plaxton himself offered to be the 'offender' and a fund was raised to indem-
nify him against any loss he might sustain. So on 6 May 1852
Plaxton threw down four feet of fencing, filled in the ditch,
and drove into the enclosure both cattle and horses. In the case
that followed this alleged trespass, the court found against
Plaxton and ordered him to pay forty shillings for damage.

This appeared to be a setback for the freeholders and commoners, but all the court had done was allow Wellesley-Pole the little bit of rope that was eventually to prove sufficient to hang both him and his fellow lords of manors. The success of his tenant, Isaac Lake, emboldened him to enter into an agreement with the Commissioners of Woods and Forests for the purchase of royal privileges over defined areas of forest land at Wanstead and Woodford, including about twenty-two acres lying between Wanstead Park, Wanstead Flats and Little Ilford, part of which was land involved in the dispute between Isaac Lake and Richard Plaxton.

As Lord Warden, Wellesley-Pole, the rake, for a consideration of £12,000 had appointed a Mr Cutts steward of his manors and steward of the Forest courts. When in 1842, at the request of Sir George Cockburn and other freeholders of the Forest, a Verderers' Court had been held, Mr Cutts had attended and claimed to act as clerk. He had continued to act as clerk, and when, in 1852 or 1853, the Verderers tried to gain possession of the records he refused to hand them over until he was paid a sum which he claimed the Lord Warden owed him. When new stewards were appointed by Lord Mornington the available records dated only from the time of George II. It seems probable that the courts fell into abeyance as the result of the unco-operative attitude of the steward when Wellesley-Pole left the country.

As time went on, the poor as well as the rich took to enclosing land, especially at Loughton, where one of the Verderers, William Whitaker Maitland, lived. The Maitland home was Loughton Hall; but after the old house was destroyed in the fire described by Dickens in *Barnaby Rudge,* William Whitaker Maitland went to live in a house adapted from the White Lion Inn at the top of Goldings Hill, an old hostelry that had lost much of its trade with the construction of the Epping New Road. All round him on Goldings, Baldwins, and York Hills were squatters who had built small cottages for themselves and had then proceeded to enclose bits of forest waste by getting a live fence, usually bramble, growing round it. Over the years this enclosure was enlarged by cutting back the bramble on the inside and encouraging it to root on the outside. For this reason it was commonly known as a rolling fence.

In estimating the social effect of these squatter enclosures we need to bear in mind that Loughton was then a small village of 1,200 souls, with Mr Maitland a typical village squire. Many responsible people regarded these cottage enclosures with favour. Families had to be fed, habits of industry were to be encouraged, and it was better that the poor should maintain themselves by cultivating small gardens and building a sty for a pig than by poaching and thieving as many had done previously. Some of these squatter families were of gipsy stock, and it seemed all to the good that they were settling down in this way. Mr Maitland himself sometimes helped those who could not afford more than a poor shack by buying their holding and building them a decent cottage on it, even although the land enclosed was manorial and he was lord of the manor.

In all, by the middle of the century William Whitaker Maitland owned 1,120 acres of cultivated land in the parish in addition to the waste. Most of this was let out in ten farms, the largest of which were Alderton Hall Farm, Bridge Farm, and Loughton Hall Farm, sometimes referred to as the Home Farm, and whatever Mr Maitland's personal views about the Forest may have been, there is no doubt about the views of his tenant farmers, which was that it was an unmitigated nuisance.

When William Whitaker Maitland died in 1861 he was succeeded as squire of Loughton by his grandson, the Rev. John Whitaker Maitland, who since 1856 had been rector, and who lived until 1909. It was during his time that London suburbs reached what in 1861 had been a Forest village with a population of 1,526. Ten years later the railway had reached Loughton and the population was 2,439; in 1881 it was 2,851; in 1891—3,880; in 1901—4,730. Most of the new inhabitants had settled round the railway station, so the Baldwins Hill neighbourhood retained its rural character, and here the new squire continued his grandfather's practice of buying squatters' cottages when they came into the market, rebuilding them, and in this way improving the living standards which were still lamentably low on the edge of the Forest, especially in the Hollow, a notorious settlement between Monk Wood and Woodbury Hill, Loughton.

Among the cottagers rehoused in this way in 1866 was Thomas Willingale, who accepted the squire's offer to rehouse him on two main conditions. The first was that he should be accommodated in a cottage in Lower Road, Goldings Hill, while his own cottage was being rebuilt; the second was that the squire should buy from him an encroachment of the waste of Epping Forest of approximately two perches, which he had added to his garden during his twenty-seven years on Baldwins Hill, and which he claimed by squatter's right. This was the Thomas Willingale who was shortly to become the champion of the commoners!

So the popular idea that all the enclosures were made by wicked landowners is as far from the truth as such one-sided notions usually are. The key to the situation was, in fact, neither legalistic, nor moral. It was simply the fact that in the middle of the nineteenth century the irresistible force of urban expansion met in this hitherto remote forest village of Loughton the immovable object of centuries-old rights and privileges of commonage. In other parts of the country many of these rights had been lost during the great enclosures of the eighteenth century simply because there had been no one at hand strong enough to fight for them. Here they had remained unchallenged until the middle of the nineteenth century, and when they were challenged they were stubbornly defended.

The confrontation between the enclosing lords of manors and commoners came in the 1860s between the rector-squire, John Whitaker Maitland, who enclosed more than one thousand acres of Forest waste within his own parish and started selling it off in building plots, and the Willingale family. The rector's action provoked the indignation of his neighbour, Sir Thomas Fowell Buxton of Warlies, Upshire, head of the great Radical family that had been associated with the liberation of slaves and the prison work of Elizabeth Fry, and when Sir Fowell, as he was known, found that two Loughton commoners were determined to fight for their rights over the enclosed land he offered them financial support. Without this support it is difficult to see how even the most determined commoners could have withstood the pressures that would inevitably have been brought to bear on them, both local and national. There was no legal aid in those days. But with that support, Thomas Willingale and another Loughton commoner named Castell filed bills in Chancery in 1866, the one claiming lopping rights, the other both lopping rights and the right of common pasture.

Once the men behind the scenes had agreed to support the cause of the commoners it must have been clear to them that Thomas Willingale was the ideal man to lead the revolt against the enclosing landowners. He was head of a family that had for years been the chief exercisers of the right of lopping. It was said that of every hundred trees lopped, eighty were lopped by Willingales, and Thomas was a stickler for starting the lopping as the clock struck midnight on the night of 11th November, because he was firmly convinced that the right would be lost for ever if no one was there to wield the axe at that precise moment. So every year, one hour before midnight on the night of 11 November, Thomas Willingale with his family, friends and neighbours assembled on Staples Hill, Loughton, lit a bonfire and waited for the appointed hour to strike.

According to a local story, an attempt was made to stop this ceremonial start to the lopping season. The Willingales and their supporters alleged that the lord of the manor invited them to a supper at the King's Head, Loughton, in the hope that by midnight they would all be too drunk to exercise their rights. Needless to say, this has always been stoutly denied by the Maitlands. The persistence of the story is only one of several allegations that were to colour the Willingale account over the years. In 1933 the Rev J. W. Hayes, then living in retirement in Loughton, interviewed Alfred Willingale, by that time an old man of ninety-one, living as most of the Willingales had lived, on Baldwins Hill, and also William Willingale, son of the Thomas who had led the revolt in the 1860s. William said that he had frequently heard his father tell the story of the supper at the King's Head, how he kept sober and at 11.30 walked out on to Staples Hill, where he lopped off a branch, bore it down to the King's Head and flourished it triumphantly before the entire company. Many local people must have had the very tree from which Thomas Willingale cut the branch that night pointed out to them. It is certainly beyond dispute that Thomas Willingale was a great character. He was a tall and impressive figure—a king among commoners—and he also had the reputation of telling a good story.

Alfred Willingale, Thomas's nephew, was firm in his conviction that the right of the commoners to lop depended on the season starting at midnight on 11 November, that it extended to the same hour on 23 April, and that lopping must be restricted to the boughs and branches above the height of seven feet from the ground. He was also firm in his conviction that this right extended to all the woods of the parish with the exceptions of Monks Wood and Loughton Piece.

Mr Hayes noted that he found Alfred and William Willingale so circumstantial about both lopping rights in Loughton and the incident of the supper at the King's Head that he personally was entirely satisfied that they were telling the truth. Fred Brand, however, a painstaking, scholarly man who compiled an 'Essex Index' which has been used by students ever since his day, was equally convinced that the story of the supper was a complete fabrication. For the Willingales it could be said that as Fred Brand served the parish church both as organist and churchwarden during John Whitaker Maitland's incumbency, he was prejudiced in favour of the rector. The Rev J. W. Hayes was a most interesting and entertaining character, who delved into all kinds of subjects, principally archaeological and occult, was learned and scholarly in his methods, but was at the same time an expansive Irishman who never spoilt a good story in the telling. It is to be doubted whether he could ever be considered a good judge of evidence.

On the other hand, there can be little doubt that the exercisers of lopping rights, no less than the exercisers of rights of pasturage, had come to be a thorn in the side of the landowners. John Maynard, schoolmaster of Theydon Bois and a native of Waltham Abbery, in a history of the Forest published in 1860, had a story about a general drunk and supper held with the same object at Waltham Abbey on 11 November. It is all very confusing, so for a more reliable account of the kind of thing that was happening we turn to Epping, where Henry John Conyers, lord of the manor, persuaded his tenants to transfer their lopping rights to him on his undertaking to cut the wood at his own expense and deliver it to them ready for use. The reason he gave for offering this service was that the Forest was becoming unsightly through indiscriminate lopping, as undoubtedly it was. By planned lopping, he argued, this could be avoided. Unfortunately, Henry John Conyers did not keep his part of the bargain. After a few years the Epping commoners were told that there would be no more fuel for them, and that if they cut any themselves they would be prosecuted because their rights had now lapsed.

The commoners of Theydon Bois came under a similar threat. "Even poor women," states Maynard, "are ordered off the Forest and threatened with imprisonment if found gathering up a few sticks; while thousands of faggots are being carted off from this part of the Forest by the lord of the manor." He adds: "There is need yet, in this highly favoured country, for disinterested and honest men to arise to the help of the poor against the power of the oppressor."

It was against this background that in November 1865, supper or no supper, Thomas Willingale, who would be over seventy years of age at the time, asserted his right to lop. The following month he appeared before the Epping Bench, with the lord of the manor, John Whitaker Maitland, in the chair, charged with injuring forest trees. The charge was dismissed. So in spite of the chairman's great interest in forestry, which was real, there does not appear to have been any prejudice against Willingale on that occasion. In the following March, however, Thomas's son, Samuel Willingale (1840-1911), with Thomas's nephews, Alfred Willingale (1843-1934) and William Higgins (1842-70), were summoned to appear before the Waltham Abbey Bench for a similar offence and there they were found guilty and fined two shillings and sixpence each, with eleven shillings costs and damages, or, in default of payment, seven days' imprisonment. The chairman was Mr. J. S. Davies, and according to a newspaper report of the proceedings he was at pains to explain to the defendants that in the opinion of the court they had acted illegally, "but as the bench only wanted to put a stop to the abuse the magistrates sitting would only impose on the present occasion a very small fine of two shillings and sixpence", together with costs. Again, this does not suggest victimization. The report of the case ends: "The defendants, who behaved with considerable levity in Court, appeared to treat the matter quite in the light of a joke, and said they would each 'do the seven days'. They were then removed from the bar and locked up." Years afterwards, Alfred, who was one of the three, said they had the money to pay but preferred to go to gaol. Each in his way became a legend. Older residents of Loughton still re-member Sam Willingale as a silent, brooding man with massive forehead and heavy jaw, sitting in front of his cottage on Baldwins Hill watching his two pet adders. When he had given them their exercise he used to slip them into a long stocking which went into the pocket-hole of his corduroy trousers and slid down the side of his leg. From time to time he would hang a red pocket handkerchief over a fence, then go behind the fence himself and jangled stones in a tin. This would excite the adders and make them spit at the handker-chief until they had emptied their poison bags. After that they would be safe in the stocking down his trouser leg. This was the family that sparked off the fight against the squire of Loughton, and that by drawing in the aid of the Buxtons eventually led to the saving of the Forest for all time.

After it had engaged the attention of the Commons Preservation Society, through the intervention of Edward North Buxton, and finally that of the Corporation of London, the long-drawn-out dispute, or series of disputes between the commoners and the lords of the Forest manors acquired the dignity of national drama, which all too often degenerated into melodrama, with Thomas Willingale in the role of the village Hampden and John Whitaker Maitland in that of the wicked and oppressive squire. Thomas Willingale was un-doubtedly well cast. Whether John Whitaker Maitland fitted the part allotted to him may be doubted. That he tried to suppress the commoners' rights cannot be denied; but there is no reliable evidence that he ever acted vindictively or be-trayed trust in the way Henry Conyers did. He certainly put a ring fence round the whole of 1,316 acres of forest land contained within his manor, leaving only fifty acres of roadside waste unenclosed; but he must have been advised that he was legally entitled to do this. Commenting on his action and general attitude, Percy Thompson, a former secretary of the Essex Field Club, who knew the rector well, said: "Those of us who remember the Rev. John Whitaker Maitland . . . will have difficulty in believing that so gracious and friendly a personality can ever, at any period of his life, have been guilty of so mean an action as that with which he is charged."

What is certain is that no one who was a party to these village arguments in the 1860s could have foreseen what they were starting. The deeper the Commons Preservation Society (later renamed the Commons Open Spaces and Footpaths Preservation Society) delved into the law relating to commons and open spaces, the more complicated the issues involved became. Years slipped by while the lawyers wrangled. Thomas Willingale himself died before his own case came up for hearing and consequently it lapsed. At one point it looked as though the Gordian knot never would be undone. The vast extent of the disputed legal territory will be indicated in the next chapter; but it will be convenient here to summarize the end of the Willingale saga. Thomas Willingale's death before his case could be heard and examined in court meant that speculation was rife and a legend was created which gained the credence of a great many persons who should have known better than to put their faith in uncorroborated evidence. Among these was a person no less eminent than Mr G. Shaw Lefevre, afterwards Lord Eversley, chairman of the Commons Preservation Society. In a letter in *The Times* of 17 November 1874 he wrote:

An old labouring man named Willingale, who for many years of his life had exercised this right, and partly earned his livelihood by cutting wood in the winter months, was determined not to submit. He persisted in the annual lopping and invited his sons and neighbours to do the same. For this act two of his sons and a nephew were summoned before the magistrates, and although they protested their right, which should have arrested the jurisdiction of the Bench, they were sent to prison for seven days, with hard labour.

The letter proceeded at considerable length to recount the events which eventually led to the Forest being won for the public. In the main it is an accurate account.

But five years later, in a speech made on the night of 11 November, as reported in the *City Press* for 15 November 1879, we find Mr Shaw Lefevre saying that for defending their rights, Willingale's "sons were arrested and convicted by the magistrates of malicious trespass to property, and were sent to gaol for three months with hard labour". The sentence had increased from seven days to three months! This, of course, was the report of an after-dinner speech and after-dinner speeches are not normally characterized by accuracy. In other words, they should be taken with a pinch of salt! No one would want to hold a slip of that kind against Mr Shaw Lefevre. But in 1894 he published a book entitled *English Commons and Forests*, in which he again describes the events leading up to the appearance in court and proceeds:

> they were convicted of malicious trespass on property, and were sent to prison for two months with hard labour. It turned out that one at least of the magistrates had received an allotment of the enclosed lands in compensation for his rights. One of the Willingale's sons was put into a damp cell in the prison, where he caught a severe cold, which developed into pneumonia, and resulted in his death.

I have shortened the account, which can, of course, be consulted by anyone interested; but in this third version by Mr Shaw Lefevre of the Willingale story, Thomas himself is among the defendants sent to prison, the nephew has disappeared, and we have the sensational addition of martyrdom. We are told that one of the sons died as the result of the penalty imposed by the wicked magistrates. This statement has no foundation in fact, and one of the three, Alfred Willingale, was at all times available to correct the account. According to him the three were handcuffed and taken to Ilford gaol. One of them did catch a chill and was said to have been seriously ill for a time. The extraordinary thing about the illness, however, is that Alfred Willingale and Thomas Willingale disagreed about which of them it was. Thomas said: "the poor man nearly lost his life, and in consequence was obliged to be a burden on his club nearly all the summer". We may think that he should have known the truth about this, because according to him the poor man in question was his own son, Samuel. Alfred Willingale denied that Samuel ever caught a chill in prison and was positive that it was William Higgins who was ill. What is certain is that William Higgins lived until 1870 and Samuel Willingale until 1911. It is fair to state, however, that descendants of William Higgins claim that his death at the early age of twenty-eight was the result of the chill he caught in prison in 1866.

What might be thought the final irony in this long sequence of well-nigh incredible events was that when Lopping Hall was opened, the Rev. John Whitaker Maitland pronounced a blessing on it, although it had been built with money paid in compensation for rights that he, in common with other lords of Forest manors, had refused to acknowledge, and of which his own Vestry had disapproved strongly only a few years earlier. But the irony may be more in our reading of the events than it was in his. Hindsight is notoriously facile. The ability is rarely given to any man to view the events of the past with the eyes of a contemporary. Hard things have been said about John Whitaker Maitland as the wicked squire of Loughton, usually by writers and public speakers who had no personal knowledge of him, and little knowledge of the facts of the Willingale case. He was a faithful parish priest who worked hard in many spheres in local life—the Bench, the Forest, the Board of Guardians, the Rural District Council, and later the Urban District Council, of which he was first chairman. Thomas Willingale himself enclosed land, and sold his enclosure to the man who, in fact, owned the soil that had been enclosed: both squire and cottager lived according to their lights, and probably understood each other better than we can understand either. Thomas Willingale was a hard-working, respectable man. He was employed by Sir George Carrol, a former Lord Mayor of London, from whom he received a small legacy.

Surely the truth is that both the Willingales and the Maitlands were caught up in a tide of events that swept them into positions that neither could have foreseen. But when all has been said that can be said about those years of bitter controversy and suspense, Thomas Willingale still remains the central figure, because it was he who stood firm when the rights of the commoners of Epping Forest were challenged, and it was his axe that struck the first blows in the fight that gained for all the inestimable boon of these 6,000 acres of beautiful woodland.

CHAPTER III

THE CORPORATION OF LONDON
INTERVENES

THE MOST significant date in the struggle to save Epping Forest
was 1854. In that year the Commissioners of Sewers of the
Corporation of London bought 200 acres of Aldersbrook
Farm to provide a cemetery for the City. The significance of
the purchase was that it gave the Corporation commoner
status, and the importance of this was seen in June 1871,
when trustees acting for Earl Cowley (Henry Richard
Wellesley) enclosed about twenty acres of waste on Wanstead
Flats adjoining the Corporation's cemetery, which by this
time was the only piece of unenclosed land remaining in the
manor of Aldersbrook. Notice was immediately served on the
Earl's trustees requiring them to remove forthwith the offending fences and gates.

If the Earl was in any doubt about the strength of local
feeling running against him, and of the Corporation's determination to mobilize that feeling, that doubt must have been
dispelled on 8 July following, because on that date thousands
of people assembled on the Flats to attend a meeting presided
over by Sir Antonio Brady of Maryland Point to express
indignation at the action of the Earl's trustees. Despite this
display of local feeling the fences were not removed. So in the
following month the Corporation instituted proceedings in
Chancery against the Earl, and not only against the Earl, but
against all the lords of manors who had recently enclosed
land.

The time was opportune. During the 'sixties illegal enclosures had engaged national as well as local attention. In
February 1863 the House of Commons had sent up an address
to the Crown praying that directions be given that no sales to
facilitate enclosures of Crown lands might be made within

fifteen miles of the metropolis. A committee of the House of
Commons had reported on the subject about the same time.
Neither had come to anything. So in 1870 the blind M.P.,
Henry Fawcett, a keen naturalist and follower of John Stuart
Mill, moved for another address to the Crown.

Meanwhile the movement for action continued to gain
momentum in west Essex, and in April 1871 Mr Cowper
Temple, afterwards Lord Mount-Temple, successfully moved
in the House of Commons:

> That it was expedient that means be adopted in accordance with
> the address presented to the Queen in February 1870, for
> preserving as an open space, accessible to Her Majesty's subjects
> for purposes of health and recreation, those parts of Epping Forest
> which have not been enclosed with the assent of the Crown or
> by legal authority.

The motion was opposed by the Chancellor of the Exchequer,
Mr Robert Rowe, afterwards Viscount Sherbrook, who when
called upon elsewhere to explain his opposition adopted the
argument consistently used by the lords of the manors, namely,
that Epping Forest belonged to the lords of the manors and was
vested in them to do what they liked with. The law, as we
have seen, was far from clear at this time. No doubt he knew
that the public had no legal rights of their own to resort to the
Forest for purposes of recreation and enjoyment, and as
Chancellor of the Exchequer he was on his guard against the
Government being called upon to purchase such rights for their
benefit. He must therefore have been angered when the motion
was carried by a majority of nearly one hundred. He was, in
fact, so incensed that in a later speech he said that the success of
Mr Cowper Temple's resolution "was treated by the government with contemptuous indifference".

The effect of this derisory attitude on one respected citizen
of London, Mr John T. Bedford, was to sting him to protest
vigorously and to bring the whole question of the future of
Epping Forest before the Court of Common Council on 25
May 1871 by proposing and carrying the following resolution:

> That a Committee be appointed to seek a conference with Her
> Majesty's Ministers, to ascertain on what terms and conditions

the Corporation can secure to the people, for purposes of public health and recreation, those parts of Epping Forest which have not been enclosed with the assent of the Crown or by legal authority.

In a sentence, he was asking the Corporation to assume the responsibility which the Chancellor had indicated that the Government was not willing to assume. His motion was carried unanimously; but, as might have been expected, the interview with Her Majesty's Ministers merely confirmed that no help was to be expected from that quarter. So the Corporation resolved to try in the courts the question of what precisely were the rights of the public over the wastes of Epping Forest, and the City Solicitor, Sir Thomas Nelson, in collaboration with Sir Robert Hunter, who played a leading role in the establishment of the Commons Preservation Society and of the National Trust, began preparing the way for the great action that was to win the Forest for the people.

The Corporation of London's interest in the Forest needs some explanation at this point. It was certainly more than manorial. One key to it was sporting. It was traditionally believed that the citizens of London enjoyed the right to hunt in Epping Forest. Curiously, no written evidence of this right has ever been found, although it was claimed by the Corporation that Matilda, wife of Henry I, built the bridge at Stratford "with the object of facilitating the access of the citizens of London to the great Forest of Essex, for the enjoyment of their usual recreation of hunting there". Against this, W. C. Waller, in an examination of the Corporation's claims printed in the *Essex Naturalist**, points out that no claim on behalf of the Corporation was ever presented at any Justice Seat where charters of privilege were allowed and enrolled. It may be doubted, however, whether this is conclusive evidence that no right had been granted. At all events, long-established tradition had it that Henry I granted the privilege of a day's hunting in the Forest of Epping to the citizens of London, and that when Henry III in 1216 granted a licence to the Abbot of Waltham to impark woods at Nazeing and Epping he at the same time renewed the privilege of a day's hunting

* Vol. viii, p. 34.

to the citizens of London within a circuit of twenty miles.

What is not in doubt is that this old hunting ground of kings and their courtiers came to be increasingly popular with London citizens who settled in the Forest parishes. In Victorian times particularly, forests became fashionable. They provided a romantic background for Victorian Gothic architecture. The improved roads, which had come about as the result of the activities of various turnpike trusts, had brought out a new leisured class into the country. Distinguished gentlemen planted avenues of horse chestnuts. Deer parks became an expected amenity adjunct to the most important great houses in every county, and as the nation's wealth increased the rich merchants and bankers of London who had settled on the fringe of the Forest, many of whom were only one generation removed from good farming stock, saw the Forest as a godsend. So riding and hunting became popular with men of a new social class who possessed wealth but not land, and who—human nature being what it is—resented the restrictions of what they regarded as the anachronistic nonsense of such claims as those of Earl Cowley and other local landowners. And as several of the most eminent of these new local residents were Aldermen of the City of London, the Lord Mayor's Hunt came to be the great event of the year in the Forest. George Palmer of Nazeing stated that the Lord Mayor and Aldermen, to his personal knowledge, had exercised the right of hunting in the Forest and killing a stag once a year for fifty years, and Alderman Copeland gave evidence of having attended Easter hunts in the Forest since 1808.

With such a tradition in mind, it may be assumed that much of the emotion engendered among the City merchants and bankers who sat on the Court of Common Council arose out of these ancient privileges being threatened. Apart from a few such families as the Buxtons, most of these champions of the freedom of the Forest were jealous of their own rights no less than of those of the commoners; but that does not lessen the importance of the stand they were taking. It is doubtful whether any local family except the Buxtons appreciated that they were doing pioneer work in a field hitherto unexplored. In the 1860s the National Trust, for example, had not been conceived. At the earliest it dates from a meeting called at the invitation of the Duke of Westminster in November 1893. It did not become a registered institution until 1895. There was no Ancient Monuments Department in 1870, no formulated policy for town and country planning. The Commons Preservation Society was in existence. It had been formed in 1865 to resist attempts to enclose large areas of Hampstead Heath and Wimbledon Common; but it was not a property-holding body. The Council for the Protection of Rural England had not even been thought of. So Mr Bedford's resolution was much more far-reaching in its effect than the Court of Common Council that passed it unanimously could possibly have foreseen.

When these matters came to the attention of the Lord Chancellor he saw at once that before the Corporation went ahead with its action it was desirable that the powers of the Verderers' Court of Attachment should be tested. But the election of Verderers had fallen into abeyance. Only George Palmer of Nazeing survived from those who had been so bitterly criticized at the beginning of the 1860s. So a writ for the election of three Verderers to fill the vacancies was issued to the High Sheriff of Essex, and Sir Antonio Brady of Maryland Point, Mr Thomas White of Chigwell, an Alderman of the City of London, and Mr Wythes of Epping were elected. The four of them proceeded to do what George Palmer had wanted to do earlier. They agreed to deal with the various complaints, and duly gave notice that they would sit for the purpose of hearing them at the Castle Hotel, Woodford, on 16 September 1871. This was the first official sitting since 1848, although George Palmer claimed that the Verderers had continued to hold courts—by which he may have meant meetings—until 1854. Locally the revival of the Verderers' Court was regarded as something of a farce. All the Forest officers were summoned to attend "as well as such of the freeholders as might have complaints to make in regard to trespass on the rights of the Queen and all her Majesty's subjects, both rich and poor, within this ancient Royal Forest, who were there to be heard in open court as heretofore".

When the court was opened a roll was called of all the last recorded officers—Master Keepers, Under-Keepers, Purlieu Rangers and the rest of them. It was a proceeding more appropriate to a seance than a court of law. The only officer to respond was an under-keeper named Robert Rounding. His appearance was greeted with laughter; but the mirth subsided when he stood up and accused the lord of the manor of Woodford of having enclosed land, because the lord of the manor of Woodford was a Queen's Counsel, and the Verderers were doubtful of their authority to pass judgement on so eminent a member of the Bar, even though Manwood had defined a royal forest as "the highest franchise of princely pleasure". A further complication was that no lawyer was allowed to plead before a Verderers' Court and the Solicitor of the Corporation of London was anxious to present to the court a long list of enclosures which he contended were unlawful. So, not unreasonably, the Verderers decided to adjourn the hearing for one month, and when the Court resumed on 26 October it was with their minds made up to retire gracefully from the scene and leave these complicated matters to be examined elsewhere.

The court had nevertheless done a good day's work. It had, in fact, heard evidence of recent enclosures involving nearly 3,000 acres, including the large-scale enclosures made by the Rev. John Whitaker Maitland since his grandfather's death in 1861, which itself was an embarrassing item because his grand-father, William Whitaker Maitland, had been a Verderer. It heard evidence of 563 acres enclosed by Robert West, lord of the manor of Theydon Bois, and among the 121 other offenders presented were the Bishop of Salisbury and Mr Ind Coope, the brewer. The competence of the court had been tested, and it had become clear to the Lord Chancellor that such proceedings were no longer appropriate to deal with such offences. Accordingly they were suspended by Act of Parliament and the Forest courts became a dead letter in Epping Forest. In August 1872, on the recommendation of a Committee of the House of Lords, all legal proceedings relating to the Forest were suspended, except the suit of the Corporation in Chancery, and Commissioners were given power to make orders abating enclosures and protecting herbage. This last was necessary, because the agent of Capt. Sotheby, lord of the manor of Sewardstone, had made plans to cut down the trees at High Beach. John Chilton, a local contractor, farmer and licensee of the Robin Hood public house, had been invited to put in a price for this; but the wrong man had been chosen. Chilton at once alerted the Buxtons—for whom, incidentally, he had no love—and the depredation was stopped.

The examining of witnesses and the making of appropriate recommendations was then entrusted to four Commissioners: Charles Wood, J. W. P. Watlington, Henry F. Barclay, and John Locke, whose main object was to make recommendations for the disafforestation (using the word in its legal sense) of Epping Forest. The time allowed them had to be extended several times, and in all they sat for 102 days, and both heard and recorded 21,853 answers to questions put to 239 witnesses, besides examining an immense volume of documentary evidence.

It was found that in 1777 12,000 acres remained unenclosed; in 1793, 9,000; in 1854, 7,000 in 1871, 3,500. From an examination of the rolls of the Court of Attachments it became clear that so long as the Crown rights remained, enclosures were to a very large extent irrelevant, because all land in the Forest was subject to Forest laws and Crown privileges no matter who owned the soil. It was also subject to commoners' privileges. But a new situation had arisen in the middle of the nineteenth century as the result of the Commissioners of Woods and Forests being authorized by Parliament to sell Crown rights. This amounted to provision for the systematic disafforestation of Epping Forest, and it had proceeded apace. Between 1854 and 1863 the Commissioners had sold Crown rights, which in effect meant sporting rights, over approximately 4,000 acres for about £18,000. This was less than £5 per acre. As it was estimated than in 1870 an acre of land unenclosed was worth £20, enclosed £180, the value of the right to enclose after the Crown rights had been abated was £160 per acre. So the land enclosed by the Rev. John Whitaker Maitland now had an enhanced value in excess of £160,000, which was a very considerable sum in 1870.

Months could have been spent on these complicated matters in Parliament, so it was just as well that this line of enquiry was overtaken by the timely action of the Corporation of London, through its Commission of Sewers, in 1871, which resulted in Parliamentary action being suspended until the Court had pronounced on the Corporation's suit, notwithstanding the fact that at the time of the suspension an Act of Parliament was awaiting the Royal Assent.

The suit in Chancery came up for hearing on 29 June 1874. It had taken three years to prepare, and by this time Lord Romilly, who had been Master of the Rolls in 1871, was dead and had been succeeded by Sir George Jessel. To meet the costs of the Action the Corporation made use of its right to certain dues in respect of the compulsory metage of grain imported into London. By an Act of Parliament of 1871 a small fixed duty payable for thirty years was substituted for the metage dues and was directed to be held by the Corporation for the preservation of open spaces in the neighbourhood of London. The hearing occupied twenty-three days and at the end of it the Master of the Rolls delivered judgement in unambiguous terms. Of the lords of the manor, all of whom were pillars of society, one a clergyman and one a Queen's Counsel, he said: "These persons have taken what did not belong to them, without the consent of the owners, and have applied it to their own purposes, and have endeavoured to support their title by a large amount of false evidence."

Much of the credit for the success of the Action must go to Sir Robert Hunter for his advice to the City Solicitor to reduce the many questions that had been discussed so heatedly to one main issue: that of intercommonage. As the result of this, it had been contended for the commoners that the cattle of each individual one of them could roam in search of grass over the entire area of the Forest. The lords of the manors, as defendants, had contended that this was not so: that each manor was a separate entity in relation to commoners' rights, and that each commoner was entitled to graze his cattle only on waste lying in the manor in which he lived. The point of this was that if it could be established that commoners' rights were restricted in this way, once the lord of a manor had come to an understanding or arrangement with his own commoners, most of whom were his tenants, he would be free to enclose and sell off at immense profit as much land as he pleased. But even when simplified the issue was by no means as clear in the 1870s as it appears to us now. In the early stages of the Action many landowners in other parts of the country had seen the contention as the thin end of a very big wedge. In the course of the hearing, however, the movement for open spaces had gained momentum, and it had come to be seen that as this was a question that would have to be answered eventually, and as it was unlikely that any other litigant as well qualified as the Corporation of London to test the matter in the courts on behalf of the commoners would appear, it was in the national interest that the case should be fought out there and then to a final determination. This, as we shall see, happened.

The finding, however, was far from being the end of the matter. If the Corporation of London was to acquire its benevolent control over the region it must own the soil. So in 1875 it set about systematically acquiring this by purchase. During this and the following years manors in the northern parishes totalling 3,048 acres became Corporation of London property, together with such Crown rights as were attached to those manors. Eventually 5,600 acres were acquired in this way and the preparatory work has been done for the final settlement of 1878, by which the Corporation became Conservators, and all illegally enclosed land was thrown back into the Forest. The effect of this was that all enclosures made prior to 14 August 1851 were allowed to stand, together with those made prior to 14 August 1871 which at that date were covered with buildings or in use as gardens attached to those buildings.* All other lands enclosed within twenty years of 14 August 1871, with one important exception, were returned to the open wastes of the Forest. The exception was the enclosure at High Beach made by T. C. Baring Esq., M.P., in which a new church had actually been built after the deadline date in 1851. This was allowed to stand and Mr Baring was appointed one of the first Verderers under the Act.

One result of this settlement was that the lands enclosed near Aldersbrook Farm in 1852 and in June 1871 became Forest again; but Earl Cowley's trustees reacquired the thirty-four acres of the earlier enclosures, together with several other pieces of land elsewhere. It was in exchange for this estate, supplemented by a payment of £8,000 cash, that the

*See page 58.

Corporation acquired from the trustees in March 1882 the 183 acres of the lakes and woodlands of Wanstead Park.

The restoration of enclosed land to the Forest was greeted with general rejoicing. On 14 October 1875 the Lord Mayor himself, attended by the Aldermen, Sheriffs and many of the members of the Court of Common Council, with an invited company to the total number of 700, travelled in state from Liverpool Street Station by special train to Snaresbrook, and from there proceeded in 150 carriages, each drawn by two horses, to Fairmead for luncheon. The Lord Mayor was presented with an album of photographs of the Forest which he placed in the safe keeping of Guildhall Library.

But it was clear from the start that the implementation of the decision by which some land should be restored to the Forest and other land remain private property would not be a simple and straightforward exercise. So Sir Arthur Hobhouse was appointed Arbitrator to settle disputes. These proved to be both numerous and bitter. They occupied more than four years of his time, during which he held 114 public meetings, many private meetings, and made 787 orders. Altogether eleven years of agitation and litigation were to pass between the commencement of the suit in 1871 and the date in July 1882 when Sir Arthur signed the award and the official map of the Forest, finally determining its boundaries at the date of acquisition.

The parishioners of the Forest towns and villages must have awaited this final determination with considerable impatience. There is, in fact, evidence of this. On 16 January 1878 about 100 artisans and labourers assembled and drove through the Forest in four conveyances, each drawn by four greys, with a Mr Burney of Loughton and Millwall, a prominent member of the Commons Preservation Society and Chairman of the Epping Forest Preservation Society, as leader. At Wanstead they divided themselves into three gangs, and armed with axes, saws, hammers and other similarly offensive weapons, set about breaking down the fences of recent enclosures with a will. At Wanstead, one mile of fencing went down before them. From there they drove to Buckhurst Hill, where they broke down half a mile that had been enclosed by Nathaniel Powell, a magistrate and strict disciplinarian, of whom it was said that he always required his large family of daughters to be present in the drawing-room of his home, Luctons, for the daily ritual of tea. Only one of the daughters was allowed to marry, and as she married a local curate, she was still able to be present when father took tea. Another half-mile went down at Loughton, round an enclosure made by Peter Gellatly, who was also a magistrate and later a Verderer. After lunch at the Crown, Loughton, they went on to open up an enclosure made at the Robin Hood, by the very John Chilton who always regarded himself as the champion of the oppressed poor in the district, and at the end of the day it was estimated that these three gangs had done two thousand pounds' worth of damage. The police took their names but made no attempt to interfere with what they were doing.

It would be impossible to reduce to the proportions that could be summarized here all the events of those exciting days. The entire social structure of the region went down with the fences. The lords of the manors were no longer lordly, the Forest officers had lost their power—their own claws had been cut. The Buxtons were under fire from the local gentry as traitors to their class; but they kept their heads and with clear-eyed determination played the kind of role on behalf of the commoners in Epping Forest that their ancestor, Sir Thomas Fowell Buxton, had played for social freedom earlier. Naturally, much mud was thrown at them and some of it stuck; but anyone who studies dispassionately the events of those years must marvel at the quiet determination that right should prevail shown by Edward North Buxton particularly, both before and after the acquisition of the Forest by the Corporation.

The seal was set on all these great endeavours on Saturday, 6 May 1882, when the Forest was formally opened to the public by Queen Victoria at High Beach. Never had such scenes been witnessed in the Forest before. The Corporation spent more than £6,000 on the occasion. Nearly £2,000 of this went on refreshments, £1,652 was paid to Simmonds Brothers, the upholsterers, £765 to Piggott Brothers for awnings. Forty carriages were in attendance at Loughton Station at 12 o'clock to await the arrival of members of the Epping Forest Committee and their ladies. One hundred

carriages were in attendance at 1 o'clock to await the arrival
of the special Corporation train. One hundred and ten were in
attendance at 2.30 to await the train bringing the Foreign
Ministers, Members of both Houses of Parliament and other
distinguished guests. The coachmen, each wearing a blue
ribbon, had instructions to carry all guests to High Beach and
after the ceremony to convey them back to London.

The Queen came by Royal Coach to Chingford, where the
station had been garlanded and festooned to receive her. The
platform pillars were entwined with clematis and roses. Red
carpet covered the paving stones and extended through the
waiting room into the station yard, which had been converted into a veritable flower show, with pelargoniums,
geraniums, azaleas, hydrangeas and roses blazing beneath a
canopy of palms. A triumphal arch bore the legend: THE
FOREST WELCOMES THE QUEEN.

The royal party, which included the Duke and Duchess of
Connaught, the Princess Louise, Marchioness of Lorne, with
their respective suites, had arrived at 3.30, shortly before the
royal train so that the scene could be fully set when the Queen
arrived. As Her Majesty stepped from her carriage the royal
standard was run up on the flagstaff, and the First Essex
Artillery, who were stationed on Forest land half a mile away,
fired a Royal Salute. After the local bigwigs had been
presented, the village schoolmaster's daughter came forward to
present a bouquet on behalf of the parish. Seating for 1,000
spectators had been provided on land adjoining the station.
Meanwhile a procession was formed outside, ready to move
away to the strains of martial music, the ringing of church
bells, and the cheers of the people.

At the head of the procession was a troop of Light Horse of
the Honourable Artillery Company, followed by a detachment
of mounted police. Then came a carriage bearing the members
of the Reception Committee of the Court of Common
Council in their mazarine blue gowns. The four Verderers
came next, with the under-sheriffs of London and Middlesex
following. Two or three carriages carried the principal officers
of the Corporation, including Sir Thomas Nelson, to whom
this must have been a particularly proud day. The Aldermen
and Sheriffs of London betokened the approach of the Lord

Mayor's dress-carriage, carrying the Lady Mayoress, attended by the sword and mace. Then came the High Sheriff of Essex, followed by the Lord Lieutenant of Essex. The scarlet coats of outriders and leading files of the Queen's Escort were the signal for the crowds along the route to start cheering in anticipation of the open carriage, which duly approached, giving the crowd a clear view of the Queen, the Princess Louise, the Princess Beatrice and the Duchess of Connaught. The Duke of Connaught, as Ranger, and the Lord Mayor followed on horseback, attended by Sir Henry Ponsonby, Keeper of the Privy Purse, and General Gardiner, Equerry in Waiting. Behind them came another royal carriage for the lords and ladies in waiting, and at the rear, the Queen's Escort.

At High Beach, by the Queen's gracious permission, Miss Victoria Buxton presented a bouquet. The ceremonials then continued. An enormous semi-circular grandstand had been constructed under a vast awning, facing out across the Lea Valley towards Waltham Abbey. In bold letters along the top ran the letters: WELCOME VICTORIA. From the middle of the grandstand projected the dais, carpeted and gaily adorned for the presentation of the Loyal Address, which ran:

> May it please your Majesty, we, your Majesty's loyal and faithful subjects, the Mayor and Commonalty and Citizens of the City of London, desire to express the deep sense we entertain of your Majesty's gracious condescension in visiting Epping Forest this day.
>
> The Royal Forest of Waltham was for many centuries a hunting ground for the Sovereign of this Kingdom. It has been reserved for your Majesty in the gracious exercise of Royal prerogative, with the consent of Parliament, for royal privilege to substitute popular right, and to dedicate these beautiful scenes to the enjoyment of your people for ever.
>
> Many difficulties which had to be overcome in bringing about this happy result are at length surmounted, and an open space of nearly 6,000 acres of almost unbroken forest scenery, extending from the confines of the Metropolis for a distance of thirteen miles, is now available for public health and recreation.
>
> As the capital of your Majesty's empire is the largest and most populous in Europe, it is fitting that its inhabitants should possess the most extensive pleasure ground.
>
> Your Majesty has already manifested a deep interest in this

wild and picturesque tract of ancient woodland by appointing his Royal Highness the Duke of Connaught and Strathearn its Ranger.

We speak on this occasion as well for ourselves as for the many thousands who attend to-day to testify by their presence their sincere and ardent gratitude for the solicitude your Majesty has always exhibited for their welfare and happiness, and especially for the gratification afforded them on this occasion by your Majesty's auspicious visit.

May your Majesty long live in the enjoyment of health and of the choicest blessings which Divine Providence can bestow, so that the many millions of your loyal subjects may continue to experience the unspeakable benefits of so beneficent a rule.

The Queen acknowledged the Address in words that remain engraved on the hearts of all who treasure this great heritage: "I thank you sincerely for your loyal and dutiful Address, and it gives me the greatest satisfaction to dedicate this beautiful Forest to the enjoyment of my people for ever. I thank you for the expression of your continued solicitude for my welfare."

CHAPTER IV

THE WILL OF PARLIAMENT

To UNDERSTAND Parliament's attitude to the conflicting interests just recorded and its eventual change of heart, we need
to start with the appointment in 1849 of a Commission to
inquire into the rights and claims to rights in both Waltham
Forest and the New Forest. In the course of their inquiry the
Commissioners were required to ascertain the bounds of these
forests, the private enclosures within them, the encroachments
and illegal enclosures affecting the forestal rights of the Queen,
and any other rights, such as rights of common. After ascertain-
ing the facts, the Commissioners were authorized to evaluate
these rights and privileges and put forward proposals for
extinguishing such as in their opinion remained valid. It was
recognized that in order to do this they would need to
examine the jurisdiction, past and present, of the forest courts
and, in the light of what they found in respect of these courts,
they were invited to recommend whether they should be
remodelled or abolished.

The Commissioners reported in 1850 in a singularly un-
helpful manner. They found that the many illegal enclosures
in both forests were directly attributable to negligence and
ineptitude on the part of the forest officers, and suggested that
the Crown should recoup itself for these losses by taking in
land from the remaining wastes without regard to the rights
of the commoners. They further recommended the removal of
the deer and the disafforestation of both forests.

These recommendations appear irresponsible to us now; but
they do at least reflect the Victorian lack of understanding of
the strength at law of commoners' rights in royal forests and
of forestal rights generally. Their significance for those who
examined the rights of commoners in Epping Forest at the

commencement of the Corporation's suit is that it was as a follow-up of the Report of the Commission appointed in 1849, commonly known as Lord Portman's Commission, that an Act of Parliament was passed in 1851 for the disafforestation of Hainault Forest, of which more than 13,000 acres had already been enclosed. The remaining wastes in Hainault amounted to between 4,000 and 5,000 acres, of which it was estimated that slightly less than 3,000 were Crown property known as 'King's Woods'. In the final settlement about 1,917 acres of these woods, containing upwards of 100,000 trees, were allotted to the Crown as compensation for lost rights, while the trees in the remaining portion were sold to discharge the costs incurred under the disafforesting Act.

In 1858 another Act was passed, under which, among other things, the nature of pasture rights in Hainault Forest was to be ascertained by a Commissioner, who was charged to give particular attention to the question of whether these rights were restricted to the parishes in which they arose or extended indiscriminately over all the commonable lands of the forest. He found that the rights of common over the wastes of Navestock and Woodford east of the River Roding were limited to the wastes in those parishes, that there was a right of intercommoning over the wastes of Barking, Dagenham, Stapleford Abbotts, Lambourne and Chigwell; but he did not find any evidence for a right of intercommoning over the wastes of both Epping and Hainault, which were effectively separated from each other by the River Roding.

It was a finding that cleared the way for disafforesting Hainault; but it is interesting to speculate on how different his finding would have been if he had started his enquiry from Epping instead of Hainault. In Epping, as we have seen, it was shortly to be established that every commoner had right of common across the entire area of Forest waste, no matter in which parish it was found, and that Epping and Hainault were merely two parts of the one Forest of Waltham, which itself was what remained of the Great Forest of Essex, and that both were governed by the same laws, administered by the same courts in precisely identical terms.

The point to note is that after the judgement of the Master of the Rolls in 1874 the question of illegal enclosures and

commoners' rights had to be approached by Parliament from a
new angle. Previously the question had been examined from
the point of view of Crown rights, bearing in mind that these
did not affect the ownership of the soil. After 1874 it had to be
examined from the point of view of rights of commonage,
which remained valid after the Crown rights had been extinguished. It was inevitable that this should come as a shock
to the lords of the manors, and other local landowners, who as
early as 1875 formed a 'Epping Forest Landowner's Protection
Society', with a membership that included more than one
land-owning gentleman who was subsequently elected a
Verderer. No doubt they took legal advice, and their case was
by no means a weak one in the early years. In a reasonably
public-spirited pamphlet which they published on the Epping
Forest question they pointed out with considerable acumen
that there were two conflicting demands affecting the future
of Epping Forest. One was the demand for dwellings for the
overcrowded parishes in the south of the Forest, the other was
the need for more space for recreation. This conflict of interests
has, in point of fact, continued to be put forward from time to
time during the whole of the hundred years since the Epping
Forest Act 1878 was passed, and especially immediately after
the Second World War, when there was strong agitation for
parts of Wanstead Flats to be taken over for housing.

On the question of recreation, the landowners were perfectly
correct in pointing out that there was no legal basis for the
use of the Forest for recreation. The Epping Forest Commissioners had conceded this. Their words were: "that
although the public have long wandered over the waste lands
of Epping Forest, without let or hindrance, we can find no
legal right to such user established in law". It is hardly
surprising that when the lords of the manors read those words
they thought it a little odd that Parliament should be taking
away from them rights for which many of them had paid
hard cash, and at the same time conferring rights on the public
for which in law there was no precedent.

Nor is it surprising that the Buxton brothers were regarded
by many as traitors to their class. Members of some of the
most liberal-minded local families publicly criticized them in
language that came near to justifying action for slander.

Samuel Lloyd Howard, of Goldings, Loughton, in opposing
Edward North Buxton's election as a Verderer stated that his
estate at Woodford, which was enclosed before the deadline
date under the Act, was "the largest permanent enclosure from
the Forest made in late years". He went on:

> He has no more moral or equitable right to retain it than those
> whose enclosures he has been so desirous to throw open. Why an
> arbitrary date, assented to by the City, was fixed by the Act,
> which excluded this particular enclosure from its operation, has
> never been clearly explained. Secure, however, in the possession of
> his still unenclosed forest, he, with true liberal instinct, indulges
> in mild communism at the expense of his neighbours, and then
> poses as the champion of the commoners and of an open forest.
>
> Sir Thomas Fowell Buxton also is permitted to retain enclosed
> a number of small pieces, making on aggregate a considerable
> area taken from the Forest, nearly if not quite equal to some
> purchased enclosures now to be thrown open.

It was a point of view that was at least understandable in
those who had to give up land enclosed within twenty years of
the commencement of the suit, and at that time the Buxtons
had not begun their long and impressive series of gifts to the
Forest, including the Knighton estate at Woodford, which
more than compensated for anything they had gained.

Fortunately for the future of Epping Forest the Corporation
of London remained single-minded in identifying itself with
the cause of the commoners. The City Solicitor appeared
before the Commissioners at Woodford on 16 May 1872, and
on his reporting the result to the Court of Common Council
he was authorized to collect as many claims to Forest rights as
he could, and to offer his services to any commoners who
wished to assert their rights.

On 9 July of that year the City Solicitor reported that the
Commissioners proposed to perambulate the Forest, define its
boundaries and view enclosures. It was then clear to everyone
that the tide had turned and that the rule of law was about to
be re-established, especially when orders were made to termin-
ate the flagrant offences still being committed in the manors of
Loughton, Theydon Bois and Wanstead. In January 1873
these orders were extended to affect the whole area of the

Forest, and in March of that year four watchers were appointed to prevent the further destruction of trees and other injurious acts. The validity of the various enclosures that had been effected during the twenty years prior to the commencement of the suit were examined by the Commissioners and a comprehensive scheme was prepared for the future management of the Forest. On 27 February 1875 the Report of the Commissioners was signed. It had as its basis the bounds laid down in 1641 in so far as these could be ascertained, but excluding Nazeing Park, the home of the Palmer family and those parts which had been enclosed before 14 August 1851.

The Epping Forest Act 1878 adopted the Commissioners' map as the authentic map of the Forest, and directed that it be deposited at the Guildhall, the Office of Land Revenue Records and with the Clerk of the Peace for Essex, with the one important difference that the colouring should be altered in the new map to show in green all the land that was open and unenclosed when the Act was passed, all the land that had been unlawfully enclosed since 21 August 1851 in pink. At all the places of deposit it was to be fully available for inspection and copying.

Under the Act the entire Forest was vested in the Corporation of London as Conservators, and for purposes of management an Epping Forest Committee was to be appointed made up of not more than twelve members of the Court of Common Council (who in practice have included two aldermen) and four Verderers. This committee was to be answerable to the Corporation of London and to a limited extent to a Ranger, who would be appointed by the Crown, and whose consent would be required in such matters as any change in the scale of entitlement to rights of pasturage, any change in the bye-laws, which the Corporation was empowered to make, and in certain matters arising out of changes in the terms of employment of Forest officers and officials. The first Ranger to be appointed was the Duke of Connaught, who at his death in 1942 was succeeded by Prince Henry, Duke of Gloucester, and he in turn was succeeded in 1975 by Prince Richard, Duke of Gloucester.

The Forest ceased to be a royal forest and all the Sovereign's rights of vert and venison were abolished The Forest courts lost their jurisdiction, and all the Forest laws and customs arising from them ceased to exist. This meant that although their title was retained, the Verderers were no longer judicial officers administering the Forest laws and exercising oversight on behalf of the Crown within its confines. They were retained in title to represent the commoners and be the watchdogs of local interests, but with no greater powers than those of any other members of the Epping Forest Committee. The first four Verderers under the Act were appointed by the Corporation, but it was provided that they should hold office only until 25 March 1880, by which time a register of commoners entitled to vote would be compiled, and in future those whose names appeared on that register would themselves choose their representatives. It was further provided, however, that the Corporation should have power to fill casual vacancies occurring between elections.

The first four Verderers under the Act were gentlemen of the status traditionally associated with the office. They were Sir Thomas Fowell Buxton of Warlies, Upshire, Waltham Abbey, Sir Antonio Brady of Maryland Point, West Ham, Thomas Charles Baring of High Beach, Sewardstone, and Andrew Johnston of the Firs, Woodford. The Register of Electors was to be in two parts, one for the northern parishes, one for the southern parishes, and no one should be eligible for election as a Verderer who was a member of the Court of Common Council or who was not resident in one of the Forest parishes.

All rights of common of pasture were to continue without prejudice precisely as they existed at the passing of the Act; but subject to the right of the Conservators to suspend them temporarily for purposes of Forest improvement, and subject also to requirements of management, such as the regulations that were made for the marking of commoners' cattle, always providing that any rules made should not be inconsistent with the Act.

The most important clauses of the Act are those which set out the conditions for its preservation as an open space. It was laid down that:

(1) Subject to the provisions of this Act, the Conservators shall at all times keep Epping Forest unenclosed and unbuilt on, as an

open space for the recreation and enjoyment of the public; and they shall by all lawful means prevent, resist, and abate all future enclosures, encroachments, and buildings, and all attempts to enclose, encroach, or build on any part thereof, or to appropriate or use the same, or the soil, timber, or roads thereof, or any part therof, for any purpose inconsistent with the objects of this Act.

(2) Subject to the provisions of this Act, the Conservators shall not sell, demise, or otherwise alienate any part of the Forest, or concur in any sale, demise, or other alienation thereof, or of any part thereof.

(3) The Conservators shall at all times as far as possible preserve the natural aspect of the Forest, and especially shall preserve and protect the ancient earthworks called Ambresbury Banks and all other ancient remains, and the Purlieu Bank, and such other Forest marks and boundaries, if any, as still exist in the Forest; and shall protect the timber and other trees, pollards, shrubs, underwood, heather, gorse, turf, and herbage growing on the Forest; and, subject to the provisions of this Act, shall prevent all persons from felling, cutting, lopping, or injuring the same, and from digging the gravel, clay, loam, and soil of the Forest.

The recurring phrase "subject to the provisions of this Act" refers to the powers of management that were conferred upon the Conservators in later sections. For example, they were empowered to enclose temporarily for purposes of improvement, to build lodges and other buildings for purposes of management, and to cut and lop trees themselves for the same purpose. Subject to these and similar provisions the public were given the right to use Epping Forest as an open space for recreation and enjoyment. Nothing in the Act is more revolutionary than this grant. As we have seen, it had been found that although the public had long wandered over the Forest without let or hindrance there was no right to such freedom of use established in law. In point of fact, the section of the Act which gave this right of use in Epping Forest is the first declaration of a right for the public at large to use an open space in Britain for recreation and enjoyment. In pursuance of this public use, the Conservators were empowered

To set apart in each or any of the Forest parishes, such parts as they think fit, for the use of the inhabitants to play at cricket and other sports, and to lay out, form, and maintain cricket grounds

and grounds for other sports, and, for the better use and enjoyment of the parts so set apart, to enter into agreements with, and
confer special privileges on, particular clubs or schools.

As we have seen, when the Bill was first drafted it became
clear that many disputes would arise over the ownership of
land enclosed within twenty years of the passing of the Act,
since the Forest to be vested in the Corporation would not be
the Forest as it existed in 1878 but the Forest as it existed in
1851, subject to hundreds of exceptions where buildings had
been erected within that period. So the Arbitrator, Sir Arthur
Hobhouse, Q.C., was given absolute and plenary powers of
settlement. His awards, which were not required to follow the
rules of the law courts, were to have the effect of Acts of
Parliament. With powers so far-reaching, it must have been a
relief to him to find that his jurisdiction did not extend to
ruling on questions of dispute between lords of manors and
persons who had acquired illegally enclosed land from them:
"Nothing in this Act shall give to the Arbitrator any jurisdiction over or authorise him to hear or determine any question
between a lord of the manor and a grantee from him." If any
owner of land enclosed since 21 August 1851 (the date of the
passing of the Act) wished to be relieved of the requirement to
restore it to the Forest he had to satisfy the Arbitrator that it
fell within one of the following exceptions:
1. That it was now built over, or formed the garden belonging to or curtilages of buildings, and this included gardens
enclosed from the waste, even if the building to which they
were attached was not itself on forest waste.
2. That by reasons of its smallness, situation, or other circumstances it was of no value to the Conservators for the purposes
of the Act.
3. That it was in use as a nursery garden on 14 August 1871.
4. That on the date of Epping Forest Commissioner's Final
Report, 1 March 1871, it was held for use as a burial ground,
a yard, a playground or other purpose in connection with a
church, chapel, school or other charitable institution.
5. That the enclosure in question had been allowed by agreement between the owner and the Corporation of London in
connection with the purchase of other parts of the Forest.

The Arbitrator was also given power to determine how much the Corporation should pay for land restored to the Forest in this way, and when the enclosure should be thrown open. All this was in respect of land coloured pink on the official map. Land coloured green automatically became part of the open wastes of Epping Forest on 14 August 1851; but as not all of it had been purchased by the Corporation when the 1878 Act was passed the Arbitrator was authorized to fix the price of the unpurchased land with the minerals thereunder and the timber thereon, and in respect of any strips of land which the Corporation regarded as being of no value to the Forest he was given authority to dispose of them as he saw fit.

Among minor rights that were to be tested and assessed by him, it was recognized that the most important and most controversial would be that of the lopping rights claimed by the parishioners of Loughton. The Epping Forest Commissioners had found in their Final Report that these rights were valid, but the Master of the Rolls had made certain observations about the alleged right as found by the Commissioners (Chilton v. Corporation of London, L.R., 7 Ch. Div. 735). In consequence of this, the finding of the Commissioners was adopted by the Act, but it was referred to the Arbitrator for final determination. In respect of these minor rights as found by the Arbitrator, the Conservators were required to compensate for any loss by payment of a gross sum or annual sums of money, or, in the case of fuel rights, by delivery to the claimant of the quantity of the entitlement. The process by which this was to be done was laid down in the Act: "The compensation or composition in respect of any rights specified in the First or Second Schedule of this Act, or any rights of a like nature, shall be determined by agreement between the persons respectively entitled thereto, or committee of such persons, and the Conservators." The procedure by which this agreement was to be reached was set out. Nevertheless, with the best will conceivable on the part of the many claimants it is clear that if the Arbitrator had not been given such absolute powers of final determination suits would have dragged on interminably. This was particularly true in respect of the rights that figured in the Willingale case; but in view of the reference of the lopping claims to the Arbitrator it became possible to reach a quick decision, and these claims were terminated with an award of £7,000, although the cottagers of Loughton had claimed £19,000. Of this sum £1,000 was distributed among the claimants and the remainder went to found a charity called 'The Lopping Endowment', for which the Arbitrator himself prepared a scheme. It was out of this fund that Lopping Hall was built as a public hall for the village of Loughton.

At the same time the fuel assignments in Waltham Holy Cross and Sewardstone were extinguished on payment of just under £13,000 compensation, which was increased by the addition of the costs incurred by the parishioners to £15,000.

Further provisions under the Act are too complicated to summarize here. It would serve no useful purpose to attempt such a summary. Obviously, the manner in which the Conservators were required to exercise their functions were specified in detail, although surprisingly little is said about the raising of capital and income to fulfil those functions. It was taken for granted that the wealth of the City would always prove adequate, and this benevolent role has been continued so unostentatiously that even today few people living in the Forest parishes appreciate their good fortune in enjoying this inestimable amenity without being called upon to contribute one penny piece to its upkeep in either rates or taxes.

The Act did, however, provide for an Epping Forest Fund to be established, the capital of which was to be made up of money paid to the Conservators for redemption of rent charges and by way of compensation from persons acquiring lands marked pink on the map on such lands being quieted in title. It was also to receive "all moneys and proceeds of all property contributed or given by any person to the capital of the Fund". But most of the capital was to come from the private wealth of the Corporation of London. The income for the day-to-day running of the Forest was to come in the main from duty which the Corporation was empowered to levy on all grain brought into the Port of London, supplemented by the income derived from the various services provided by the Conservators for which a charge could be made. In the early years the cost of running the Forest was trifling. For the year ended 31 December 1881 the amount contributed from the

City's Grain Duty Fund was a mere £2,000. The net cost today is well in excess of one hundred times that amount.

The powers of the Corporation under the Act were very extensive indeed; but during the first years of management there was a certain amount of anxiety about how they should be exercised. In 1880 an Act was passed extending the Arbitrator's powers for a further period of two years and giving the Conservators power to exchange portions of Forest land for other land if the Arbitrator was satisfied that the exchange would be beneficial to the public as well as to the owner of the land to be acquired. This appeared to some critics to be opening a very wide door which might be used in favour of the landowners rather than of the public at large. Fortunately it was only available for a very short period, and during that period it was unquestionably used for the benefit of the public. It was under these powers that Wanstead Park was acquired. Another valuable acquisition was at High Beach, where Fairmead Lodge and the six acres of Hill Wood behind it were acquired. This particular acquisition meant that there would be no enclosed land between Queen Elizabeth's Hunting Lodge at Chingford and Paul's Nursery at High Beach, which did not come back into the Forest until 1920. More than £128,000 was expended by the Corporation on the acquisition of land after the passing of the Epping Forest Act 1878. The total cost to the Corporation of the acquisition of Epping Forest and Wanstead Park, including expenses of management to the end of 1882, was £286,159 19s. 4d. At this date it was estimated that the annual expenditure, including the Superintendent's salary, the wages of thirteen keepers, and £2,000 for labourers' wages, would be £5,522.

Finally, there was the election of four Verderers by the commoners of the Forest parishes to succeed those nominated under the Act. Four gentlemen were nominated for the northern parishes, three for the southern. In the north, the two sitting Verderers, Sir Thomas Fowell Buxton and Mr Thomas Charles Baring, were joined as candidates by Edward North Buxton and the Samuel Lloyd Howard of Goldings, Loughton, who made such a savage attack on the Buxtons and disputed their claim to be fit and proper representatives of the commoners, although he sat with them on the County Bench.

1. On Woodbury Hill near Loughton

2. Queen Elizabeth's Hunting Lodge

3. Forest weatherboarding

4. Little Monk Wood

5. High Beach church

6. Pollards on Shelley's Hill

7. Forest deer

8. Chingford Plain

9. Election of Verderers (the author is speaking)

10. High Beach

11.   View across the Roding Valley

It was a complicated quartet. Edward North Buxton was not opposing his brother, so he was asking the commoners to elect two members of one family. The situation appears to have arisen through uncertainty as to whether Mr Baring would stand. If he didn't it was obvious that in the opinion of the Buxtons, Samuel Lloyd Howard must be kept out. In the event the two Buxton brothers were elected, and in Edward North Buxton the Forest gained the finest Verderer it has ever had. Throughout his forty-four years in office he was always the commoners' man; but the commoners were not always behind him in his battles with the Corporation on their behalf. He supported the Corporation and its officers when they were under attack locally, but the Corporation frequently found that he was a thorn in their side, and he was not infrequently a thorn in the side of the Superintendent, whose business it was to see that the Corporation's instructions were carried out. In any fight, Edward North Buxton was always in the front line, yet he remained at all times benign, patient and self-assured. And, as those who worked both with him and against him would add, he usually got his own way in the end.

In the south the election proceeded without rancour, although Andrew Johnston was himself a cousin of the Buxton brothers. A man of great wisdom and character, he enjoyed universal respect and would frequently be called upon to mediate between Edward North Buxton and the officials of the Corporation. Sir Antonio Brady, his fellow candidate, had been prominent in the fight to save the Forest. They were challenged unsuccessfully by David John Morgan, of Blake Hall, Wanstead; but when Sir Antonio Brady died in the following January, David Morgan was appointed in his place in accordance with the Corporation's right to nominate Verderers to fill casual vacancies between septennial elections.

CHAPTER V

THE COMMONERS REMAIN MILITANT

WITHIN A few years of taking over control it became apparent to the Conservators that the Forest was being overgrazed. They had adopted, as a temporary measure, the regulation made by the Court of Attachments in 1790, namely:

> that the Reeves within their limits, shall mark for every person that hath right of commoning on the said Forest, two cows for four pounds *per annum* rent, or one horse and no more, and so proportionate for a greater rent; but such Reeves may mark for every poor cottager, having a family and right of commoning as aforesaid, one horse or two cows, although such person does not hold four pounds *per annum*.

This was the rule in force when the Forest was handed over to the Corporation; but the 1878 Act had provided that, with the consent of the Ranger, the Conservators could substitute any other scale of value "appearing most advantageous for all the commoners".

On the recommendation of the City Solicitor the Conservators decided that the qualification for the right of commoning should be the ownership or occupation of half an acre of old enclosure unencumbered by buildings. The authority for this measure was an arbitration by Sir Horace Davy in 1883, which appeared to the Conservators to be reasonable for Epping Forest. So in October of that year the Epping Forest Committee recommended to the Court of Common Council that power be sought from Parliament to make an annual register of commoners with this qualification, and that this registration should be conclusive evidence of entitlement to depasture cattle on the Forest. In addition to this they invited Parliament to withdraw the right of parish vestries to nominate Reeves, and to vest the appointment in the Corporation.

A Bill was drafted in which sections three and four read:

> No person shall be entitled to depasture any animal in the Forest
> or to exercise any commonable right in or respecting the Forest,
> whose name is not for the time being on the Register of
> Commoners as settled by the Conservators and such register as
> settled for the year in which each septennial election of Verderers
> takes place shall be conclusive evidence of the persons entitled to
> vote as commoners thereat.
>
> Section 29 of the Act of 1878 is hereby repealed, and from and
> after the passing of this Act the Reeves and assistant Reeves (if
> any) shall be appointed by the Conservators.

The Conservators were convinced that it would only be by
obtaining full control over the appointment of the Reeves that
they would be able to ensure consistency in marking over all
the twelve parishes in the Forest region. Enquiry had shown
that in the three northern parishes of Epping, Theydon Bois
and Waltham Holy Cross the marking was already in line
with the intentions of the amending Act; but that no such
control was exercised in the southern parishes. Of the 245
persons whose cattle had been marked in these parishes, only
sixty occupied as much as half an acre of land. In order to get a
complete picture of the position a count was made on 25 July
1884 of all the animals turned out on the Forest. It showed that
of the 336 horses 150 were marked, 186 unmarked; of the 474
cows, etc., 353 were marked, 121 unmarked. The Superintendent and the Keepers were immediately authorized to remove
and impound all unmarked cattle as a first step towards controlling the grazing. This resulted in a rush to the Reeves to get
the unmarked cattle marked, and when this was refused to
those who lacked the half-acre qualification there were angry
scenes and not a few scuffles. The Loughton Vestry put forward the suggestion that instead of requiring each applicant to
establish a claim the Conservators should themselves place on
the Register of Commoners the name of every ratepayer holding a £4 rental. This could easily be done by consulting each
rating authority. But the Solicitor replied that in his opinion
the Conservators had no power to make such a register until a
reasonable time before the next septennial election of Verderers.

As an interim measure, the Superintendent was authorized to enquire into the circumstances of each case, and allow the Reeves to continue to mark for those persons whose cattle had been marked for several years past although without legal entitlement. Even this was found to cause hardship, because many of the owners of unmarked cattle were among what were then termed 'the deserving poor', while a majority of those whose horses were marked were making a business of hiring them out for profit during the summer months.

Percy Lindley of Loughton disputed the legality of the entire exercise. He pointed out that the 1878 Act provided that "all rights of common of pasture and of common of mast or pannage for swine on or over Epping Forest, as they exist at the passing of the Act, shall continue". Nowhere had the Act mentioned the half-acre qualification. As for the Corporation gaining full control over the appointment of Reeves, this was resented everywhere. A Commoners' Defence Association was formed to see "that the small commoners are not denied their birthright at the hands of the powerful Corporation, which acts too often as though Epping Forest was part of its private estate". What galled the poor commoners most was that while they were forbidden to turn out their beasts as they had done before the passing of the Act, and as their fathers had done before them, legally or illegally, well-to-do City merchants and bankers, who were settling in the Forest parishes in increasing numbers, were acquiring rights that many of them had no intention of exercising except for the purpose of voting for Verderers. It seemed ironic, they argued, that the sons of Thomas Willingale, who needed to supplement their meagre incomes by turning out the odd cow or pony, were denied the right for which their father had fought.

Edward North Buxton made it plain that his sympathies were with the cottagers, not with the Corporation officials; but he was at pains to attend meetings and expound both points of view. To a meeting of angry commoners he explained that Sir Horace Davy's ruling was based on his finding that the ancient right of commoning depended on the occupation of land by the commoner, so that during the fence month he would have somewhere to put his beasts. Sir Horace Davy's words were: "With regard to the claim by prescription, that would, of course, be a separate claim by each individual, and depend on the evidence of user in each case. But, independently of this difficulty of proof, I do not think that a claim of common of pastures as appurtenant to a house without land, can be maintained in law." The Conservators, said Mr Buxton, argued in defence of their adoption of the half-acre measure that if all the cottages with less land turned out the Forest would soon be ruined by the influx of cattle.

Against this, the cottagers in their evidence contended that such fears were groundless, since "the bare idea of poor cottagers being able to buy a horse, two cows, or a pig, for the, at best, indifferent feed to be found in the Forest" was too absurd to require serious refutation. They were not interested in either what the lawyers thought or what their arguments were. They had been used to turning out their animals on the Forest and no one was going to stop them.

To the unrestrained delight of the audience, Mr Lindley dismissed the explanations put forward by Mr Buxton, and asserted that nothing he had heard had altered his view of the passage in the 1878 Epping Forest Act on which his colleagues based their claim. Mr Buxton said that as he was not a lawyer he could only say that the law appeared to him to be as Sir Horace Davy had stated; but he agreed that it could not be disputed that for a long time it had been the practice to allow certain poor cottagers in the parish of Loughton to turn out two cows and a horse, although they did not have the half-acre qualification. Whether this established a right or not he could not say. It might well be that it was a privilege held by courtesy, and nothing more. He asked the audience to believe that the Verderers had done their best to discover whether any kind of prescriptive right existed in favour of poor cottagers in this particular parish, and they had been unable to discover any evidence for it. In the absence of this the Conservators could not be expected to grant special privileges to the cottagers of Loughton and refuse them to the cottagers of other Forest parishes. His advice, however, was that if they could not accept Sir Horace Davy's opinion they should either apply for a writ of *mandamus* or ask for the question to be examined by a committee on which the commoners had equal representation with the Conservators. He would support this personally, because he was as anxious as anyone to get the matter settled.

Heated passages followed as Mr Lindley poured scorn on the suggestion that they should go to law: "To go to law against the greatest Corporation in the World! Were they lunatics?" Mr Buxton interrupted to say that he utterly repudiated having suggested that the commoners should fight the Corporation. A clergyman present then proposed that Mr Buxton's suggestion to submit the case to law be adopted; but he failed to find a seconder. Order was eventually restored, and at the end of the meeting a vote of thanks was actually passed to Mr Buxton for his attendance.

Powerful support for the Commoners' Defence Association came from Lord Rookwood, who as Sir Henry Selwin Ibbetson, Member of Parliament for Epping, had piloted the Bill that became the Epping Forest Act 1878 through the House of Commons. At a meeting of the Association he stated that although he was not a lawyer he did know what he had had in mind in drawing the Bill, and two things had been in the forefront: one was Sir George Jessel's decision on the rights of the commoners, the other was the report of the Commission that had sat for two years to decide upon a course of action without, however, reaching any final decision. He said that he drew the Bill upon the decision as to the law as it then stood, and he knew that it was the intention of the fifth clause that it should provide for every owner and occupier to have the right of common from the very fact of his occupation. He went on: "It might be said that the Corporation of London, which had paid large sums, was entitled to make bye-laws for the regulation of the Forest. Yes, but the limits of those bye-laws were laid down in the Act: they referred to specific objects, and nobody could by a bye-law abrogated a clause of the Act." Therefore, although he was no lawyer, he hoped, as the man who drew the Act, that its intentions would be carried out.

The Secretary of the Commoners' Defence Association brought this statement by Lord Rookwood to the notice of the Lord Mayor, pointing out that the statement showed that it was clear that in his lordship's opinion "the owners and occupiers of lands and tenements lying within Epping Forest are entitled to be placed on the Register of Commoners in accordance with Section 5 of the Act, which preserves to the Commoners 'all rights of common of pasture, of mast or pannage for swine, as they exist at the passing of the Act, etc'." He asked the Lord Mayor to use his influence with his fellow Conservators to see that justice was done. Meanwhile the Ranger intervened personally and for the time being the proposals for amending the Act were withdrawn.

But this was far from being the end of the story. Despite Edward North Buxton's concern for the poorer commoners, there was a growing feeling among them that the new residents in the Forest parishes were anxious to change the character of Epping Forest. They needed a voice of their own class on the Epping Forest Committee. John Chilton came forward as their nominee. In 1887 he published a pamphlet declaring that the Epping Forest Act 1878 had been "ruthlessly broken to suit the interests of local wealthy despots by threatened litigation and tyranny to suppress the small Commoner's right of electing his own representative". He produced what he alleged was evidence of class prejudice in the attitude of the Conservators to local planning, and charged them with dealing with Forest problems not as trustees, holding the Forest for the benefit of the public, but as businessmen with an eye to a profit. He instanced a quarter of an acre of land adjoining Queen Elizabeth's Hunting Lodge at Chingford, which had been sold for hotel stabling. He alleged that there had been an attempt to enclose and sell the village green at Chingford which had only been stopped by the timely intervention of the Rector, and as an instance of the Conservators' attitude to development in the interests of the ordinary people of the district he cited what had happened opposite Queen Elizabeth's Hunting Lodge. There a small enclosure in the possession of the Lord of the Manor, the Rev. Robert Boothby Heathcote, had been let to Mr John Riggs, "the well-known Contracting Caterer", on a building lease; but no sooner had the building been commenced than a Bill in Chancery was filed against the Lord of the Manor and Mr Riggs for attempting to cross twenty paces across the land of the Forest with building materials. The Defendants gave way, and the Freehold of the Lord remains a nullity against improvement". Another example of influential Verderers—the

Verderers were always blamed for what went wrong—obstructing access to building sites of which they disapproved was to be seen on the south of the Green at Theydon Bois.

Mr Chilton was a valiant champion of the poor commoners, but in trying to follow some of his arguments it is necessary to remember that he wore more than one hat. As a building contractor he was far from being disinterested, and was sometimes naïve enough to complain of injustices being perpetrated when others were carrying out work for which he had unsuccessfully tendered.

Meanwhile the overgrazing continued. As a compromise, Edward North Buxton persuaded the Conservators to compile two registers, one of legally qualified commoners, the other of persons allowed to turn out one horse and two cows as an act of grace; but these two lists only showed how wide the gulf was between those who were entitled to vote for Verderers and those who stood most in need of commoning rights.

As letters to the Corporation from the Commoners' Defence Association on the question of qualification produced no satisfactory answer, a question was asked on behalf of the Association at a meeting on the Court of Common Council which resulted in the *Evening News* reporting:

> Mr. Brookman asked the City Solicitor whether his attention had been called to an article in *The Evening News and Post* headed "Epping Forest Scandal", and whether it was true, as stated there, that the Corporation, as Conservators, had been persistently endeavouring to take away from the smaller commoners the right of Pasturage, which was alleged to be theirs by immemorial right, and sanctioned by the Epping Forest Act 1878. Mr Brookman asked further whether the assertion reported in the same paper was true, that orders had been given to the Superintendent, Major McKenzie, to refuse to mark the cattle of cottagers who had less than half-an-acre of ground attached to their cottages.

The City Solicitor replying on behalf of the Corporation, described the charges as "wholly groundless". That he did not explain the distinction between those whose cattle were enlarged by entitlement and those by act of grace may not be surprising, as by this time it had been held that the Corporation had no power to allow privileges of this kind to those who were not legally entitled to them. It was, however, unfortunate that he went on to say that Major McKenzie had nothing to do with the marking of cattle, because although he did not personally superintend the marking he did hand to the Reeves the list of those whose cattle they should mark. What should have been said was that Major McKenzie was not responsible for compiling the list. Perhaps the Corporation adopted the motto: "Least said, soonest mended".

When a Mr W. C. Willmore of Forest Gate applied to have his name placed on the list, the City Solicitor pointed out that the applicant had not sufficient land to keep cattle during the Fence Month, and that the application could not for this reason be entertained. On this the Commoners' Defence Association commented that the Fence Month was as dead as the dodo, and quoted Edward North Buxton as saying: "from ancient times it has been held that to have the right of a commoner, a man must hold land to maintain his animals during the Fence Month. When the Corporation became Conservators they fixed the amount of this at a minimum of half an acre". But he had also said: "I was stating an historical fact, not advocating the revival of the Fence Month at the present day."

The truth was that the acceptance of the principle of allowing cattle on the Forest as an act of grace had caused the City nothing but embarrassment.

While these matters were being discussed so heatedly the number of £4 households in the Forest parishes was increasing rapidly. The third quarter of the nineteenth century was a period of unprecedented expansion in West Ham, Leyton and Walthamstow, as thousands of terraced houses of late nineteenth century style still show. When the estimated figure of these reached the hundred thousand mark it was plain to everybody that the number of cattle being turned out was so greatly in excess of the limit the available pasture could sustain that the starved condition of Epping Forest cattle during the winter months became a scandal. When this came to the notice of the law officers of the City they were not slow to point out the folly of allowing privileges that had no foundation in law. Edward North Buxton's personal stock was low. Finally, each of the Reeves was handed a list of those who were entitled to turn out, and they were told to turn away all who had enjoyed the privilege as an act of grace.

The Corporation again decided to seek parliamentary aid in dealing with a situation that had become intolerable, and in 1891 a second attempt was made to get the 1878 Act amended to provide that the presence or absence of a name on the List or Register of Commoners should be conclusive evidence of who were and who were not commoners, and only those who had the half-acre qualification should be entitled to registration. Again the Buxtons opposed the City over this, Edward Buxton going so far as to offer to bear the full cost of having the legality of this restriction tried in the courts. Only when advised on high authority that the result of such an action could not possibly be in doubt was he persuaded to withdraw.

When the Corporation's intentions became known the Commoners' Defence Association, on 9 May 1891, wrote to the Lord Mayor, giving him the names of Loughton cottagers who had turned out for periods varying from twelve to thirty years who were now to be refused what they had regarded as their birthright. One of these was John Willingale of Woodberrie Hill, Loughton. In the same year another member of the Willingale family wrote personally to the Conservators: "As Mr Dean [the Loughton Reeve] refused to mark my cattle at the last marking day, I should feel obliged if you would kindly have my name placed upon the list of commoners, in order that I may continue to enoy the same right which I have had for a great number of years."

Faced with local criticism, Edward North Buxton wrote to the *Woodford Times*:

The notion that the existing Verderers have trampled on the rights of the Willingales will seem rather laughable to those who know the inner history of the notable case connected with their name. I know very well that the influence of my colleagues as well as my own has always been used in the direction of the extension of the privileges of poor men as far as is compatible with the law, rather than their restriction. As a matter of fact, the elder Willingale was allowed to turn out his cattle, and one of his sons remains on the list with the same privilege.

He continued to attend public meetings, no matter how bitterly he expected to be criticized, and to maintain his attitude. At a meeting held in 21 December 1892, as reported in the *Woodford Times* of the 23rd, he said that

> he and his brother Verderers were most anxious to do the best they could for those who were least able to help themselves, viz. the poorer members of society, not only in that parish but other parishes as well. He would much rather that the privileges of commoners were used by poor people instead of by the well-to-do; they needed their privileges the more, and it gave him sincere pleasure when he knew that they gave little people an advantage.

Again the Corporation had to withdraw, this time on the vigorously expressed objections of two members of the Corporation itself, Mr A. C. Morton, M.P., and the redoubtable Deputy, John T. Bedford.

CHAPTER VI

THE FOREST UNDER MANAGEMENT

THE OBLIGATIONS of the Conservators were not confined to defending the rights of commoners. They held the Forest in trust as an open space for the recreation and enjoyment of the public. Most of it was anything but open in 1878. The best parts were out of reach of any except the most determined. So the first concern of the first Superintendent, William D'Oyley, and his staff of keepers under the direction of the Epping Forest Committee (which had John T. Bedford as its chairman) was access. That the construction of roads should have been given priority is understandable when we know that William D'Oyley was a Loughton surveyor, who claimed in his application for the post to know the Forest and its capabilities well, having resided in it the greater part of his life, and to have had "extensive professional experience". In planning and improving roads he concentrated first on the needs of those who travelled from East London in pony traps or donkey shays, or who came by rail to Loughton or Chingford Stations with the glades between Chingford Plain and High Beach as their destination. This involved both repairing old roads and constructing new ones. Palmer's Bridge Road was the first to be drained and ballasted. Then Hawksmouth was improved along with the road from Chingford Station, which had been started by the joint enterprise of the Corporation and the Great Eastern Railway Company, and was now extended. Whitehall Lane was repaired; but as this was carrying traffic from Chigwell and Loughton as well as from the East End, a new road was cut at Corporation expense from the Hunting Lodge to the Woodford-Epping road. On being opened by the Duke of Connaught it was named Ranger's Road, which became doubly appropriate when

76

Connaught Water was formed to the north of it.

The Green Ride was the next major work. It was designed to provide, as the name implies, a green ride through the most beautiful parts of the Forest for a distance of approximately six miles between Chingford and Epping. Other rides and glades were opened up, the best of them following the lines of ancient trails first trodden by pilgrims to the Holy Cross at Waltham, or by the monks of Waltham Abbey when they came out to serve the various chapels-of-ease, which were built as daughter churches when the parish system was established. The glades radiating from Fairmead Oak and Grimston's Oak date from these early years of management, as does the path from Staples Hill Pond by way of Debden Slade, Loughton Camp, High Beach, and along the Verderers' Ride to the top of Woodredon Hill. Another glade, twenty feet wide, was cut through scrub from Buckhurst Hill cricket field to the foot of Warren Hill, Loughton.

Drainage was William D'Oyley's next priority. Much of the Forest was so swampy that it was impassable for pedestrians and useless for cattle most of the year. Many of the watercourses had been blocked for years, causing swamps that were so dangerous that they might become a serious liability to the Corporation if not drained quickly. So some of the surface water was cleverly drained into ponds, which proved popular not only for their scenic value but also for boating and fishing, and to provide drinking water for cattle. This gave the Conservators the idea of constructing a large lake to drain Fairmead, where the land recently opened up to the public was permanently swampy and covered with rushes. In this condition it provided very indifferent pasture for the commoners' cattle. So everybody was pleased when this project was embarked upon. Moreover, there was the Ching Brook to feed it, and these various factors combined to enable the Conservators to construct in Connaught Water a lake eight acres in extent, which proved so popular that in 1893 it was enlarged and further improved by the construction of additional islands.

Among other notable ponds on which major work was carried out at this time were the Old Warren Pond opposite Queen Elizabeth's Hunting Lodge, the gravel pit at Sandpit

Plain at the foot of Baldwins Hill, Loughton, and the Wake
Valley Pond, which had been formed when clay was excavated for the road in 1830. The pond at Goldings Hill was
cleaned out and enlarged. Turning to the southern part of the
Forest, a disused brickfield on the north side of Wanstead
Flats was converted into a pond, and a series of large holes
and gravel pits near Whipps Cross were connected to form a
pond. These gravel pits had been heavily worked by Mr
Bosanquet of Leytonstone, who received £800 in the arbitration awards for loss of income. The pond opposite the Eagle
at Snaresbrook received special treatment after Sir Henry Peek
had shown the Conservators what had been done for Caesar's
Well on Wimbledon Common. The Eagle Pond had already
been enlarged from an ancient spring known as Birch Well,
which was supposed to have healing properties and may well
have been the original well from which Wanstead got its
reputation as a spa.

The Conservators' attention then turned to the trees, particularly those on the Loughton manor, where lopping had
been so severe. So thinning was undertaken on Staples Hill as
an urgent necessity. Elsewhere the places in greatest need of
thinning were at Chingford, where so many new paths had
been laid, and in the neighbourhood of Ambresbury Banks,
close to the Green Ride.

The Forest management had now entered on a new phase.
The roads and ponds had been planned by the first Superintendent, whose reign was brief, although the work was not
completed in his time. On 18 December 1879 he was succeeded by Alexander McKenzie, and the long reign of the
McKenzies opened. Alexander was succeeded by his son,
Francis Fuller, who in turn was succeeded by his son until
1949, when Alfred Qvist was appointed. Francis Fuller
McKenzie was Superintendent from 1893 to 1932. He died in
1957, aged ninety-two. It is some indication of the respect in
which William D'Oyley, the first Superintendent, was held
that he was asked to continue to advise on matters connected
with arbitration for a further year.

The most important building in the Forest then as now
was Queen Elizabeth's Hunting Lodge at Chingford. It had
been occupied for many years by a family named Watkins,

who had been Under Keepers paid by the Crown for a period of 120 years. The last of them was appointed a Keeper by the Corporation, and, as will be mentioned later, when he died his widow became first caretaker of the Lodge museum.

When the Corporation took over there was no shortage of labour available for either major or minor works. Mr Watkins was not the only Under-Keeper paid by the Crown under the old system to be taken on as a Keeper by the Corporation. The post proved so popular that when the Conservators first advertised for staff, 200 men applied for six jobs. One of the attractions then as now was the occupation of lodges with a rural setting yet well placed for urban amenities. Several lodges were built in those early years: two at Earls Path, Loughton, two at Woodredon Hill, two at Bushwood, Wanstead, and one at Epping. For these, half-a-crown a week was deducted from the Keeper's wages. For other Keepers, cottages were bought at Loughton and Woodford.

Among successful applicants was the first of the Luffmans, who were to give good service over many years, and the first of those well-remembered Keepers, Butt, father and son, whose memories of the Forest were recounted by Fred Speakman in *A Keeper's Tale*. After the half-crown for the cottage, the wages were twenty-three shillings a week. This was sufficient in the late nineteenth century to attract men of fine character who took great pride in their work. They established a tradition that has been maintained throughout the hundred years that have followed. No doubt much of the credit for the respect in which the Epping Forest Keepers have been held has been due to the high standards set by the three McKenzies who succeeded each other as superintendents, and later by Alfred Qvist. Of those first six keepers, J. Chellis and F. Luffman were appointed Head Keepers, J. C. Barber, Henry Butt, W. Hawthorn and J. Nield Under Keepers. The next trio to be appointed were Charles Watkins, Isaac Neale and Henry Saunders.

The Epping Forest Act authorized the swearing in of Keepers as Constables. For a time the Corporation hesitated about adopting this, but improved access had made the Forest more popular with the ever-increasing population, not only of the East End, but of 'London over the Border', as Dickens called the eastern suburbs. Eventually it became necessary to augment the services of the uniformed Keepers with those of plain-clothes Constables of the Metropolitan Police Force during the summer months in order to keep a check on the gipsies, vagrants and the various classes of unruly persons habitually seeking cover in the Forest, many of whom lived rough.

There were many nuisances to be abated in those early years. The Lopping Settlement did not immediately solve the problem of cutting trees in Loughton. On 11 November following the award a number of men assembled on Staples Hill as usual and proceeded to lop the trees. Seventeen of them were taken before the magistrates at Epping and fined five shillings each, including costs. When this was announced at the next meeting of the Court of Common Council, a recommendation was adopted that having vindicated the law there should be no process to enforce the fines if no further cutting took place. This advice was accepted; but when on 11 November 1881 eleven persons were found lopping, they were charged with the offence and fined two pounds each plus costs, with a sentence of imprisonment stipulated in default. When this was done the deterrent proved effective and no further lopping was reported.

Another nuisance that continued was the indiscriminate digging of gravel by surveyors of highways. The Act had prohibited this except where the Conservators gave their consent, or where, in default of this consent, an order had been obtained from the Justices, who in giving consent were empowered to prescribe the conditions of working, and to require the surface to be restored. It was probably under-standable that after years of laxity it took time to bring these diggings under control. So it was with many other nuisances. Even the newly constructed ponds were used as places in which to dump dead animals and refuse.

Deer stealing was rampant in those days. Few, in fact, were left when the 1878 Act was passed; but the Keepers were so vigilant that by January 1883 Head Keeper Luffman was able to report that the herd was approaching the hundred mark. Most of the old entitlements to free venison disappeared when the Forest was disafforested, that is to say, when it was freed from the operation of the Forest Laws. But the Conservators agreed with the lords of the northern manors to deliver two bucks in summer and two does in winter to the rector-squire of Loughton, the Rev. John Whitaker Maitland; one buck in summer and one doe in winter to Capt. Sotheby of Seward-stone; and the same to the lord of the manor of Waltham Holy Cross, Sir Hereward Wake. But vigilant as the Keepers were over all these Forest affairs, they needed byelaws to make their supervision fully effective. So in 1880 a set of byelaws was approved by the Ranger for the entire area of the Forest.

These byelaws were administered reasonably and came to be respected by most people. They provided among other things for the provision of entertainment on a wide scale, and this brought applications to erect swings, booths and coconut-shies, as well as to allow donkeymen to ply for hire on the Forest. In the early 1880s, the increase in population, together with the new facilities provided, created problems of control for the most popular of the traditional Forest events, the Easter Monday Hunt. In 1882 it was alleged that the crowds attending it were so large, and the resulting drunkenness so scandalous, that the whole event was a complete farce, devoid of sport, which must be abolished.

So it was not only the Conservators who had problems to face during those early years. The officers of the law were at full stretch, and not all the acts of vandalism were against the Corporation. Some were in favour of that august body. The charge that attracted most attention was that brought against the Mr Burney of the Commons Preservation Society who, as reported earlier, anticipated the 1878 Act by taking the law into his own hands and leading out a gang to break down the fences round illegal enclosures before they had actually been declared illegal. Although the police had taken no action at the time beyond taking names, several actions were sub-sequently commenced against him in Chancery, which put him to the expense of £1,369 18s. 6d. This was brought to the notice of the Corporation with a plea that as his action had materially influenced public opinion in favour of throw-ing open illegally enclosed land a contribution towards his costs should be made from City funds. As it was believed that he had acted in good faith, albeit illegally, he was granted £650.

Perhaps the one blot on the record of those first four years of hard work was the discovery that £366 15s. 5d. out of monies paid for the quieting of titles had been misappropriated by the Arbitrator's Chief Clerk.

Wanstead Park added to the problems of those early years. Large sums of money had to be spent on making it suitable for recreation. Parts of the Ornamental Water were foul with sewage that had come in from the River Roding, the paths were choked with undergrowth, the fences broken down and the buildings in a state of dilapidation. When these had been attended to, a broad walk, eight feet wide, was cut to connect the existing paths in order to give the public a continuous gravelled walk. The Ornamental Water was enlarged. Both Heronry Pond and Perch Pond were made suitable for boating, the Ornamental Water being reserved for wild fowl and herons. All this had been accomplished when the park was opened officially on 1 August 1881.

One enterprise of those early years that was not pursued was the extension of the Great Eastern Railway to High Beach, for which the Court of Common Council gave its assent in 1881. This was planned with the laudable intention of enabling visitors to reach High Beach; but when angry critics, led by Sir John Lubbock, protested against its intrusion into the beautiful glades across Fairmead the scheme was dropped.

Those who are constantly worried by the high cost of capital works today must marvel at the amount accomplished within the limits imposed by a £6,000 a year budget in those early years. It is true that in 1883 the estimated expenditure was exceeded by more than 50 per cent; but the £9,792 expended that year included exceptional expenses related to the official opening by the Queen in May 1882 and the large-scale work that had to be undertaken during the first year in Wanstead Park. For a short time Wanstead enjoyed an unexpected income from the Grotto, which was opened to the public in December 1882 and attracted thousands of sightseers. But this came to an end when it was destroyed by fire on 20 November 1884. It was a unique building that could not possibly be reconstructed in its original style, so all thought of replacing it was abandoned and the Superintendent was instructed to make the ruin as picturesque as he could and leave it at that.

Inflation was not a problem in those days. When the Corporation took over, the situation of Superintendent was advertised at a salary of £500 a year with a free residence. Alexander McKenzie was only getting £600 a year when he died in 1883 after thirteen years in the office, and his son was appointed to start at the original figure. Hawkwood Farm (Jubilee Retreat) was bought in 1880 for £1,200 to provide an official residence for the Superintendent. But it was occupied by a farmer named Gunn, and was subject to a lease that had six years to run. This was surrendered after less than half that term had expired; but the McKenzies had taken up residence at The Warren, which has remained the official residence of the Superintendent ever since. All the outbuildings at Hawkwood Farm were transferred to The Warren, and Hawkwood farmhouse became the residence of Head Keeper Foster. The name of the farmhouse was changed in 1887 to celebrate the Jubilee of Queen Victoria. It was then a 'Retreat'. Another building acquired in those years, Fairmead Lodge, which had been a refreshment house since 1853, was let to a Mr Bartholomew who catered extensively for parties of schoolchildren visiting the Forest. The house was bought with a view to its demolition, but it was serving such a very useful purpose that it was allowed to remain for some years.

Labourers were engaged to do most of the thinning, which had to be stepped up year by year, and which, as we shall see in the next chapter, came to be bitterly criticized by those who had too romantic a view of Nature and what she can accomplish unaided. When the Forest came into care it was obvious that if healthy growth was to be re-established practically the whole of the surviving woodland would have to be cleared. The difficulty was to decide where to begin, bearing in mind that too drastic a clearance in one area would expose the adjacent woodland to sudden and dangerous exposure and increase the risk of fire. It was also well in the minds of the

Conservators that temporary disfigurement of the parts cleared would provoke criticism. Loughton was the manor most in need of treatment, but this was the most sensitive area because of the abating of the lopping rights, and Loughton cottagers were always the most militant. If they saw timber being cut and sold at what they believed to be a profit—although it never was—they would again be up in arms against the wicked Conservators. So it was decided that thinning should be spread over a wide area and continued over the years with a view to a permanent programme of thinning in rotation—the programme that is still followed in keeping with the system initiated immediately after Edward North Buxton became a Verderer.

In 1880 the Superintendent had three separate small areas at Chingford, in the vicinity of Hawkwood and Bury Wood, cleared so that the public could see the kind of treatment that was in mind for the whole of the Forest. This was inspected by the Epping Forest Committee and fully approved. The following winter the programme was put into effect and resulted in the following work being accomplished during the 1880s:

1881-2—Scrub round selected large and promising trees on Fairmead and near Ambresbury Banks was cleared.

1882-3—Dense undergrowth was cleared and trees thinned in parts of Walthamstow Forest, Honey Lane Quarters, Hawkwood and Bury Wood.

1883-5—A number of serious fires alerted the Conservators to the danger of these being even greater than they had thought, so during these years all forest work was directed to minimizing the effect of these where the danger appeared to be greatest by clearing away as much dead wood as possible from the undergrowth.

1885-6—Theydon Wood and the Lower Forest at Epping were thinned and cleared of excessive underwood.

1886-7—One hundred and fifty acres at Clay Rise and north of Broadstrood, Loughton, were thinned, which was modest treatment in view of the expert evidence given before the Arbitrator when he was considering the value of the lopping rights in this parish, that in the 721 acres of woodland in this parish there were an average of 160 pollards* to the acre, and

*Lopped trees.

that in some parts there were as many as 800.

1887-8—About 360 acres extending between Loughton and Waltham were thinned.

1888-9—Again the work extended over 360 acres, or there-abouts, starting with Kate's Cellar and the Hole, Loughton, and moving east to Debden Slade, north to Ambresbury Banks, and south-west to Gilbert's Slade, Walthamstow.

1889-90—Saw lighter thinning over a very extensive area, including Hawkwood, both sides of Ranger's Road, at Ching-ford, Fairmead, Earl's Path, Loughton, and High Wood, Theydon Bois.

All areas thinned during these years were visited by the Committee before the work was started, and when at the end of the period of ten years the Committee returned to inspect the first places thinned they were heartened to see over large tracts a healthy new growth of oak, beech, and birch which promised well for the Forest of the future. They had also gained enough knowledge of forestry in the region, which by common agreement was to be developed in the interests of amenity and never of profit, to formulate the following principles:

1. Each annual thinning to be spread over an area of about 500 acres of thicket, which is to be gone over lightly, and that no blackthorn or undergrowth be cut, except where it is dead or necessary to be removed for the improvement of the growth of neighbouring trees, or for protection from fire, or for the purpose of felling pollard trees.
2. The pollard trees to be removed are to be marked with a 'tree slicer' by the Superintendent.
3. Young healthy seedlings to be selected and given adequate room to grow, especially in those blocks of the Forest where there are no 'spear' trees.
4. The stems and faggots to be removed without delay, and with as little injury as possible to the green rides.
5. A set of uncoloured Ordnance Maps (25 in. scale) to be obtained, and the areas to be thinned marked thereon by the Chairman of the Committee, with the date of the Order.

During the winter of 1888-9 an average of thirty-two men were employed over a period of fifteen weeks in thinning, which by the end of the ten years since the Corporation embarked on the programme had gained such momentum that criticism had become vocal. By 1890 the gangs of wood-men engaged on this work were being watched by observers who at the beginning of that year wrote in such critical terms that on 1 May 1890 the Epping Forest Committee was in-structed by the Court of Common Council to prepare a report answering their criticisms, and also dealing with other allegations of excessive thinning currently appearing in the Press.

The Committee reported that throughout the Loughton manor lopping had been carried out so ruthlessly prior to 1878 that no tall trees of any age had survived. In other parts, however, pollarded areas had recovered, and in some of these so dense a growth of thorn now covered the ground with impenetrable thicket that there were few paths, and what survived were narrow and swampy. In some parts the stunted trees had been allowed to remain so close that when they sprouted a dense canopy was formed which made it impos-sible for sufficient light to penetrate. Most of these lopped trees were rotten at the core because water had lodged in the crowns. Their life was short, and new growth must be en-couraged if they were to be replaced. It was not, however, proposed to clear them away entirely. Small groups would be left as picturesque features of the Forest and to show what the trees were like when lopping was in full swing.

Most of the criticism came from new residents who had built villas in Loughton and Buckhurst Hill following the extension of the railway to those places. So the Committee were much relieved when the man who knew the district best and had least cause to be favourably disposed towards the Conservators, the Rev. John Whitaker Maitland, the squire and rector of Loughton, who was an acknowledged authority on forestry, wrote complimenting the Committee on its work. He recalled that twenty-five years earlier the whole of Theydon Forest had been thinned in a similar manner by the then lord of the manor, Mr Hall Dare. There had been an outcry from the village even then; but the result of the thinning was the magnificent growth of beech to be seen at Theydon Bois, which now needed the treatment repeated. When he himself had thinned Monk Wood he had been threatened with an injunction, and had purposely left a portion of two or three acres unthinned near the Goldings Hill to Wake Arms Road, intending to return to it later. It never was done and now the trees were past cutting. They had been drawn up to reach the light, and the lower branches died off through lack of light and air.

From the beginning the intention was to provide conditions that would promote natural regeneration and make planting unnecessary; but during the first ten years some planting had to be done. Some of the land that had been enclosed before 1851 and was now back in the Forest had either been stripped or trees had been cut indiscriminately, leaving hard, unnatural lines. So planting was undertaken on a considerable scale. Most of these plantings were in the south, and not all were respected. Among the first to be planted was an avenue of black Italian poplars along the road across Wanstead Flats from Forest Gate to Wanstead. About 200 of these had to be replaced in 1883 and 300 more by the end of 1884. Thirty-five were destroyed by vandals in one night. In all, 56,000 young trees were bought at the beginning of the 1880s for planting in denuded areas. Little was needed in the north except to screen new building development, particularly at Theydon Bois, where the former lord of the manor, despite what the Rev. John Whitaker Maitland said, had gone too far, notably on Piercing Hill. In the vicinity of the churchyard, planting was done to screen the Plain from the devout, and at the other end to screen Riggs Retreat. In 1886 the Poplar Avenue on the eastern side of Woodford Green (which had to be cut down in 1966) was planted. In the same year 40,000 trees were planted over about twelve acres of Wanstead Flats, which during these years was being drained, levelled and sown with grass. Drainage had to be done everywhere in order to provide the right soil conditions for healthy growth.

Another angry protest flared up when on 26 March 1889 a party of gentlemen entered the Forest at 9.30 a.m. with guns and remained there on a jay shoot until 5 p.m. Among the party were Alexander McKenzie, his son, Francis Fuller McKenzie, two members of the Barclay family, four members of the Buxton family, Mr Pelly and Mr Whitbread, the brewer. The sound of shots fired brought out the locals, who became increasingly vocal as the day went on. Recently, they alleged, a Keeper on an estate adjoining the Forest at Chingford had been prosecuted for shooting a stoat. Did Mr McKenzie and his friends consider themselves above the law? Edward North Buxton and two of his sons were members of the party, so it was hardly surprising that he should have been reminded in the Press later that in his book on the Forest he had said: "We owe the preservation of the forest to the fact that it was formerly kept for the free range of beasts of chase, and it is fitting we should pay them every attention. The greatest care, therefore, is taken to guard them from molestation. Guns are not allowed to be used. The result is seen in unusual fearlessness, especially of many of the birds." He was clearly vulnerable to attack. Two other Verderers, Sir Thomas Fowell Buxton and Andrew Johnston, had said much the same thing. Even more pertinent was the fact that Sir Thomas Fowell Buxton was not of the party, and it was widely reported that he was opposed to the shoot and had forbidden his sons to take part in it. Peter Gellatly, another Verderer, was critical. So, as might be expected, were most of the naturalists.

Finally, in this initial state of quite astonishing energy, came the tidying up of boundaries and the purchasing of new land, in which again the Buxtons played the leading part. In 1889 they bought and presented to the Corporation for inclusion in the Forest fourteen and a half acres at Oak Hill, Theydon Bois, which had been Forest up to 1842, but was enclosed in that year by the lord of the manor, who intended to build himself a house there. He had, in fact, enclosed all the Forest waste in the parish about 1857, but the Oak Hill enclosure was the only part he had been able to retain. The rhododendrons to be found in this bit of Forest survive from the plantation he was making in what was to be the garden of his residence. In 1890, Mr Courtenay Warner, High Sheriff of Essex, agreed to sell for £6,000 thirty acres of Highams Park to be thrown into the Forest. Towards this purchase price Edward North Buxton persuaded the Walthamstow Local Board to contribute £500, the Woodford Local Board £250, the Buxton brothers, Mr Henry Ford Barclay and others gave £2,500, and the Corporation found the rest. On 6 June 1891 the Park was opened to the public by the Ranger, and at once proved a popular asset, particularly when the lake, upwards of a quarter of a mile in length, was prepared for boating.

Seven years later Edward North Buxton wrote to the Lord Mayor inviting the Corporation to accept the gift of twenty-eight acres of Yardley Hill, Sewardstone. In his letter he said:

> I have for a long time past been impressed with the importance, if not the necessity, of securing the picturesque vantage ground known as Yardley Hill as an addition to Epping Forest ... From its prominent position it commands many miles of the valley, along which a manufacturing population is steadily assembling, as well as such distant points as Hampstead, Barnet, and the high grounds near Broxbourne. A more practical consideration is that it would connect that charming outlying portion of the Forest called Gilwell Lane, at present, owing to its isolation, rarely visited, with the main block near Hawkwood.

Yardley Hill was dedicated to the use of the public as part of Epping Forest on 1 June 1899, and again the ceremony was performed by the Duke of Connaught as Ranger. In 1902 Edward North Buxton's son, Gerald, continued the family tradition by purchasing and presenting seven acres of land at Bell Common, Epping, and the waste along the Ivy Chimney's Road.

Other odd bits were either given or purchased during those first years. In 1899 a small piece of land on the bank of the Roding away from Wanstead Park was purchased from the Earl of Mornington in order to control the flow of water from the river into the Ornamental Water. A piece of land measuring just over thirteen acres adjoining Yardley Hill was bought by the Corporation about 1890, and gradually the Forest area was built up from the 5,530 acres of the official map of 1882 to the present 6,000 acres.

CHAPTER VII

"WOODMAN SPARE THAT TREE"

ON 21 APRIL 1883 Professor G. S. Boulger, President of the
Essex Field Club, and Mr A. J. Burrows, both Fellows of the
Linnean Society, toured the Forest in the company of Sir
Thomas Fowell Buxton, Edward North Buxton, and a third
Verderer, David John Morgan. Mr W. H. James, M.P., of the
Commons Preservation Society, was also a member of the
party, but it seems unlikely that Mr Alexander McKenzie was
with them, because if he had been he would have been able
to deal with certain criticisms of forest management that the
two learned naturalists expressed in an article which appeared
in the issue of *Forestry* for June of that year. Both expressed
surprise that so little planting had been done in the parts they
visited. They regretted the lack of variety of species, which
they attributed to the lopping that in recent years had been so
savage that only the fittest trees had survived. Mr Burrows
was in favour of a very wide variety being introduced after
decayed trees had been thinned out, although he thought that
in some places the thinning already done had been too drastic
and referred to the region round Ambresbury Banks as "an
abomination of despoliation".

Professor Boulger was only in favour of species indigenous
to the Forest being planted, but thought this would provide a
wider variety than might be supposed, and he listed those he
would have expected to be indigenous in the past. He
thought the opening up of rides had been a good idea, but in
his opinion they had been cut too straight. Some of the drains
introduced he thought unnecessary in view of the many
watercourses provided by Nature, and ditches near roads were
both ugly and dangerous. Gravel digging had obviously been
excessive in the past. He was glad that it was now allowed

90

only for the repair of highways, but he had been shocked to see pits sunk close to valuable trees which had been undercut in the most reckless manner.

These criticisms went down very badly with the Superintendent, who in the following month issued his reply in a pamphlet entitled 'Epping Forest and its Management', in which he described the observations of Messrs Burrows and Boulger as "the hare-brained chatter of irresponsible verbosity". He described the Forest as it was when the Corporation took over. "It would scarcely be possible," he said, "to use language too strong when describing the lamentable condition in which they found the whole Forest." Lopping had been carried out with such vigour "that scarcely a tree of any importance was to be found". Between these scarred and mutilated veterans were thick masses of dead undergrowth in a highly inflammable condition. In fact, forty acres had been ravaged by fire in a single year. He could not believe that anyone qualified to speak as conservators on forestry, and he did not include his present critics in that description, would disagree with the opinion that the most urgent need was to remove dead underwood, clear out shapeless and diseased trees, open up glades and rides, drain the soil and free the watercourses in order to prepare the way for new and healthy growth. This, with the construction of roads needed for access, would absorb all the energies of his staff for many years. Yet despite the priority that must be given to these works, use had been made of gravel pits to provide several small ornamental sheets of water, and a larger one to be named after the Ranger, the Duke of Connaught, which was then under construction and might have been thought worthy of comment by visitors who took upon themselves to assess the value of work in progress in the Forest.

The following month the *Gardeners Magazine* joined in the discussion. Epping Forest, the writer asserted, had been going to ruin for centuries. Mr McKenzie's feelings were understandable, but he had committed himself to a two-fold mistake: "In the first place, he need not have replied at all, for his work will reply for him in due time, and indeed is making ample reply even at the present moment. In the next place, he might have been content with offering a few explanations of matters of fact, instead of which he hits too hard." He should have understood that the kind of wholesale destruction going on, however necessary, was bound to cause alarm. "Men have a right to be suspicious when they see the axe at work in a public place, for ignorance and jobbery together have wrought as much mischief in woodlands as in churches." Nature would vindicate Mr McKenzie in due course. In the meantime he should have left his critics to fight among themselves, knowing that it was inevitable that experts would disagree as they did in recent articles, in which one had pleaded for the undergrowth to be cleared because the risk of fire was so great that the entire Forest could be destroyed, another insisted that Nature should not be interfered with in any way whatever, but should be left to achieve her own purposes in her own way.

Support for Alexander McKenzie's description of the Forest when the City took over could have been found in an article in the *Cornhill Magazine* for March 1864, in which the writer stated that in the Loughton woodland not a single tree had escaped lopping. "They are not," he wrote,

> strictly speaking, trees at all, but strange, fantastic vegetable abortions. Their trunks, seldom more than a foot or eighteen inches in diameter, are gnarled, writhed, and contorted, and at about six feet from the ground, just within reach of the axe, they spread into huge overhanging crowns, from which spring branches which are cut every other year or so, and never long escape the spoiler; then, baffled in their natural instinct to grow into branches, the trees throw up spurs and whips from their roots, and every pollard stump—more or less rotten at the core—is surrounded with a belt of suckers and of sprew.

Confirmation for such descriptions is to be found in contemporary photographs and sketches, yet the critics persisted undeterred and in the spring of 1889 long articles appeared in the *Evening Post* alleging that during the previous six years 90,000 trees had been sacrificed in the thinning programme summarized in the previous chapter. Edward North Buxton was by no means disheartened by this attitude. While defending what had been done in the unusual circumstances that had obtained, he welcomed the wish of the people to preserve the natural aspect of the woodland and resist any attempt to turn Epping Forest into parkland. "The general opinion," he wrote, "so unmistakably evinced, that the Forest shall remain a forest and not be civilised into a park, is but the expression of a true instinct." The same point of view, stated philosophically without regard to the special conditions in Epping Forest, was again expressed by such learned gentlemen as Professors Boulger and Meldola. Professor Boulger recommended that "no flowering plant, shrub, or tree should be uprooted on any pretence, or by any person, and that no timber tree be felled unless within three yards of two other trees". In no circumstances was the divine right of Nature to pursue her course unimpeded to be questioned. Professor Meldola denounced the thinning as landscape gardening, and said that the Forest would remain beautiful only so long as Nature had full sway.

These were the first rumblings of the battle that has been going on ever since, namely, the conflict between those whose first concern is the natural aspect of the Forest, which the Conservators are under a statutory obligation to preserve, and those who want the whole place opened up for recreation and high jinks. Both have been constantly in the minds of the Conservators, who have done their best to maintain a reasonable balance between the two. In order to do this they have welcomed rather than deplored clear statements on both requirements, even when they have wished that each of the contending parties could occasionally see the other's point of view.

The naturalists always had at the back of their minds in those days the credentials of the Superintendent, Alexander McKenzie. From the day of his appointment they questioned whether he was the right man for the job. Alexander McKenzie had first made his mark as manager of the Alexandra Palace, where he had been "the hero of a hundred fights in the ever-changing battleground of horticultural exhibitions". He had designed and planted Finsbury Park and the Victoria Embankment Gardens. In a word, he was a landscape gardener, not a forester. It was feared that in his hands Epping Forest would rapidly become Epping Park.

In April 1894 a well-timed effort was made to deal with the academic critics. They were taken round the Forest by the four Verderers. The occasion chosen for this was a visit to the

Forest by the Essex Field Club, and members of the Epping
Forest Committee were also there to see how the Verderers
acquitted themselves before their critics. The party made its
way to Monkwood, which according to what had been said
by the Willingales had been excluded from lopping rights.
Edward North Buxton showed the company that this was far
from being, as had been claimed, a piece of virgin forest. It
had been pollarded in precisely the same manner as other
parts of the Forest, one leading branch being left on each tree.
All round them were pollarded trees that had never been
allowed to develop fully. Overcrowding had forced them up
unnaturally and had weakened them in the process. Many
were diseased and were the source of disease in others. He
pointed out those that were obviously infested with blight,
and argued forcefully that the only rational way to deal with
such a situation was to open up areas to light and weather so
that the natural regeneration which was the object to which
all their endeavours were directed could assert itself. The
result of the visit was well expressed in *The Essex County
Chronicler*, which had a paragraph: "If we were asked to state
the sum and substance of our conclusions upon the examination of the Forest, we should say at once that we think there
has scarcely been any justification for the fierce attack which
has been made upon the Verderers." When Alexander
McKenzie read this he may well have felt that the Verderers
were not the only persons who had suffered from indiscriminate attacks. There were certainly times when he appeared to get a disproportionate amount of blame and less
than his share of credit for what was done.

At a meeting of the Essex Field Club following the visit
Professor Meldola admitted that in 1883 he had said:

> To the naturalist—and I am sure I may say to the intelligent
> public generally—such a tract of primitive country is beautiful
> only so long as Nature is given full sway, and the adjustments
> which for long ages have been going on slowly and silently
> under the operation of natural laws remain unchecked and
> uninterfered with by man.

He now qualified this by allowing that this ideal "natural
condition" did not exist throughout Epping Forest, and he

saw that it had been the policy of the Verderers to arrest this unnatural interference with Nature and restore the trees to their natural condition. It might be thought that he could have seen this six years earlier if he had done more walking and less talking.

Professor Boulger joined in this chorus of contrition. He now saw that he had been wrong in criticizing the Conservators for excessive thinning. They had been given the unspeakably difficult task of regenerating a Forest all but destroyed by the vandalism of generations and they had had no precedents to guide them. He went on: "It was unreasonable to expect to see the Forest made beautiful in a year or two, and at the same time to allow nothing to be done to bring about such a result." But he still disagreed with Edward North Buxton in believing that the Forest could be regenerated by encouraging a succession of nursery crops in the hope that thorn would spring up through heather and forest trees through thorn. This, however, is what has happened, and Epping Forest is probably unique among English woodlands in relying almost solely on natural regeneration promoted by the means initiated in those first years of management.

Despite the success of this visit of the Essex Field Club in April 1894 the Conservators decided to consult forestry experts with a view to getting independent opinions on what they were doing. These gentlemen were asked to consider the question "solely with regard to the preservation of the natural aspect of the Forest, and not to the commercial value of the timber". The result was a complete vindication of the policy that had been adopted so far. Their advice for the future, which was incorporated in a Report dated 7 June 1894, was:

1. That vistas should be cut and judicious clearings made to open up the beauty of the Forest and the surrounding countryside to visitors. Such a clearing at Honey Lane Quarters would open up a view of the Lea Valley.

2. That provision should be made for the regular cutting back of encroaching vegetation along the rides. These were a beautiful feature of the Forest and should be kept open. New glades should be cut, but where possible this should be done without sacrificing fine trees or groups of trees.

3. Pollarded hornbeams were so characteristic a feature of the

Forest that undoubtedly some should be kept. The question was how many. In the opinion of the consultants, to continue the present policy of thinning the pollarded hornbeams lightly would be to perpetuate the existing monotony of the areas in which they predominated and prejudice the future. It was difficult to see what value there was in this, since at best their life was short, and if bold clearances were not made soon there would be no trees coming along to replace them. Their only value was as museum pieces, and the retention of a few strong specimens would be sufficient for this need to be met.

4. Edward North Buxton's strongly held views on natural regeneration appeared to be sound. "The natural vegetation is so luxuriant that there is little need of the planter", and in principle artificial planting should be avoided, although there might be small areas where it was desirable to scatter the seed of trees indigenous to the Forest.

5. No foreign trees should be introduced.

6. Small ring plantations should be avoided. They would be out of keeping with the character of Epping Forest.

7. The encouragement of undergrowth should be selective. In some parts it was of value, both for its own beauty and for the protection of saplings; but it would achieve nothing under the beeches, which produced a canopy so dense that it did not allow of healthy undergrowth and it should be recognized that "the effect of the closely-massed forest trees constitutes a beauty in itself".

8. They failed to see the need for artificial drainage except for rides and low-lying open spaces. Elsewhere the natural drainage of slopes and streams already there appeared sufficient, and it was important that the existing streams, channelled over the centuries by natural agencies, should be left to follow their own courses.

They then proceeded to apply these principles to specific areas in terms that were almost entirely consistent with what the Conservators were already doing. But the critics were not to be silenced. When thinning operations were resumed in the following winter another protest meeting was held, this time at Wanstead, already well established as a socially conscious residential suburb. The meeting culminated in a resolution calling on the Conservators, "in the interests of the preser-

12. The Wake Valley Pond

13. A Forest farm

14. Fairmead

15.   Theydon Bois Golf Course

16. The Epping road near the 'Robin Hood'

17. Log sawing

18. A Forest fair at Chingford

19 & 20.　Forest
drinking fountains

21. An old pump

22. Corn metage post, Jack's Hill

23. Charcoal burners' hut at the Cuckoo Pits

vation of the natural aspects of the Forest", to forgo any further thinning of living trees for a period of five years. Happily, by this time the results of what may be called the Buxton policy were everywhere apparent.

What is abundantly clear throughout these disputes about the management of the woodland is that Epping Forest was a strongly emotive subject. A whole book could be written on the different ways in which different social groups reacted to it. The naturalists had one reaction, the sociologists, who saw the need for open spaces for recreation, had another. There was the snob reaction of the new residents who saw it as a romantic amenity to their neat new villas. In an amusing letter written by John Hunt of Lippitts Hill, it was suggested that three interests predominated and could best be met by leaving things as they were, because each of the three groups favoured different parts of the Forest and it was big enough for all. There were the poor East Enders, who annoyed the more respectable by their drunken revels. They had their favourite resorts and were not a great problem. He might have added that anyway they were the people for whom Epping Forest was primarily intended as an open space for pleasure and recreation. There were the tradespeople who came out for family picnics. They favoured the quieter places with just sufficient open space for their children to play on. Finally there were the carriage folk who came out for more genteel pleasures under the greenwood tree. They stepped down from their conveyances, assisted by the family coachman, "with harp etc., and then the little dainty toes peep out from under their dress". They generally chose the High Woods. But of all these interests the strongest and most vocal was what might be called the Old Guard—the long established cottage folk whose families had depended for their livelihood on the rough grazing to be found on the Forest wastes, on the birds and animals that could be poached from the woodlands for their pots, and the wood that could be cut or picked up on the Forest floor for their winter fuel. The fact that the Forest had remained uncultivated meant that in their attitude to any sort of progress they were generations behind even the most rural communities to be found elsewhere in south-east England. As for the new commercial interests, these had no meaning for them beyond the advantage they got from the big houses of the City merchants and bankers in which their daughters could find domestic employment and their sons jobs as gardeners and coachmen. What right had anybody to interfere with the Forest that had been theirs longer than anybody could remember? These people were always ready to pack public meetings and protest against what was going on whether they understood a word of it or not. Not one of these groups was impressed by what the experts called in by the City said. What did they know about Epping Forest?

In this atmosphere it cannot have been without design that several of the most eminent and respected Essex gentlemen were invited to visit the Forest and say what they thought about what was being done there. Their support for the Conservators might be said by the cynic to have been a foregone conclusion, but still, several of them were the kind of gentlemen the local people of those days didn't mind touching their caps to. Among them were the High Sheriff of Essex, the Chairman of the County Council (Andrew Johnston, who was, of course, a former Verderer), the Mayor of Chelmsford (Frederic Chancellor, who was widely respected as a church architect), William Cole (the founder and honorary secretary of the Essex Field Club), F. Caruthers Gould, Sir Robert Hunter and the former critics, Professors Boulger and Meldola. They urged the Conservators to persist in their present policy and from their personal knowledge of the Forest testified that it had greatly improved since the Corporation assumed control. This was quickly followed by support from even more influential gentlemen, who presumably had not been able to attend with the others. These were the Lord Lieutenant (Lord Rayleigh), Sir John Lubbock, Col. Lockwood, Professor Fisher, and the President of the Essex Field Club (David Howard).

It might almost be felt that the Conservators were overdoing their defence. Need they, for example, have taken quite so seriously the criticism that erupted at Baldwins Hill during the 1894-5 thinning with the cutting of trees between Ash Green and the Epping New Road to open up the Clay Road? On this occasion the critics were so out of touch with the change that had come about among the learned that they actually quoted what Professors Boulger and Meldola had said in 1883, entirely ignorant of the fact that these two professors, who had come to scoff, had remained to pray, that Professor Boulger had admitted that the opinions he had expressed in 1883 were based on imperfect data and insufficient knowledge, and that he now thoroughly approved of the management. Yet in face of this, the Epping Forest Committee visited the areas criticized twice during the May of 1895—on the 4th and 11th—and although they failed to find any justification for this latest outburst they met seven of the complainants on the 13th of the month and undertook to invite those who had reported favourably on the Forest the previous year to return so that the experts could say whether the cutting at Clay Road, which was in implementation of their advice, had their approval. Needless to say, it had.

It is interesting to find so little agitation for the introduction of new trees into Epping Forest. This again is evidence of the overwhelming desire to keep this ancient Forest that stirred such deep emotions unchanged in character. There was, however, one eminent naturalist who had different views. This was Alfred Russell Wallace of Hertford, the man who anticipated Darwin's theory of evolution. He knew the Forest well, and was tremendously excited by the idea of having a Forest dedicated to the use of the public. Like many others who had taken Epping Forest for granted, he was under the mistaken belief that common land had common ownership, and confessed that he had read with astonishment the finding of the Epping Forest Commissioners that "although the public have long wandered over the waste lands of Epping Forest without let or hindrance, we can find no user right established in law". Now, however, it was to be managed for the use of the public, and this provided the most wonderful opportunity for "a great arboricultural experiment, attractive alike to the uneducated and the scientific".

His proposals for the future of Epping Forest first appeared in the *Fortnightly Review* for 1 November 1878. Later they were developed and published as a pamphlet. He started from the point of view that the trees in the Forest were in so decayed and wretched a state that they were not worth preserving.

This, he argued, gave the Conservators the unique advantage of being able to start the whole process of establishing a forest from scratch on soil that had already borne trees and was perfectly conditioned to repeat the process. Wallace had travelled widely and studied forests in all parts of the world. He had seen scores of new species that might be introduced into England and here was the perfect opportunity for doing it. Moreover, the idea of introducing new varieties into Epping Forest was not as new as it might appear. Dr Fothergill had established at Upton a magnificent botanical garden surrounded by shrubberies, which were themselves surrounded by a wilderness of trees. Only Kew could be compared with it. Gilbert Slater in the second half of the eighteenth century had laid out gardens at Knotts Green, Leyton, with trees and shrubs from the East, including camellias, hydrangeas, magnolias and China roses. These experiments, both of which had been successful, could now be extended over these thousands of acres to establish woodlands that would be the wonder of the world. He proposed dividing the Forest into sections, each to be devoted to trees and shrubs which were natives of one or other of the forest regions of the temperate zone. Into one section magnolias, tulip trees, red and yellow horse-chestnuts and a host of other flowering shrubs and trees would be introduced. Another section would be planted with American and Canadian trees, particularly with maples that could add to our own autumn colours their brilliant scarlets and crimsons. He was especially keen about bringing to England the great trees he had seen when collecting material for his best-known work, *Travels on the Amazon,* and prophesied that vast numbers of people would be interested in such an experiment and be fascinated by its progress,

> and as time rolled on, and one kind of tree after another arrived at its period of blossoming, and displayed each succeeding year in greater perfection its glowing autumnal tints, the "American forest" would become celebrated far and wide, and would attract visitors who would never think of going to see the more homely beauties of a native woodland, and still less a young plantation of common trees.

There would also be an Asian section, and he went on to

enumerate all the trees he would bring into the various sections from every quarter of the globe. They would come from China and Japan, from Chile and Patagonia, from Australia and New Zealand, and over the tallest trees he would have had a riot of climbing plants: clematises, Japanese honeysuckle, yellow jasmine and wistaria.

Edward North Buxton was a widely travelled man. He must have known of Alfred Russell Wallace's views. Did the two ever meet? Wallace was never a member of any of the parties of distinguished naturalists whose views were invited after being shown round and entertained in the best traditions of Forest hospitality. The two would never have agreed; but Boulger and Meldola didn't agree in the early days, yet they were entertained and won over. All we can say is that Alfred Russell Wallace's proposals were never considered officially.

CHAPTER VIII

COCKNEY PARADISE

BY THE end of the century it must have been plain to everyone that for better or worse the public liked Epping Forest being the kind of place it was and intended to keep it that way. What it was from the naturalist's point of view has been discussed. It was no less important that the Conservators should know what it was to those who resorted to it for pleasure and recreation. To gain this knowledge it was only necessary to visit Chingford Plain any weekend or, better still, on an Easter Monday, Whitsuntide or August Bank Holiday. No matter what the weather might bring, thousands of cockneys on pleasure bent bundled themselves out of trains or wagonettes from early morning till noon. Some of the mums were already smelling of gin and my-dearing everybody as they waddled out of the station yard, followed by their bairns like proudly clucking hens with their chickens fluttering along behind them. The men of those days tended to be as stunted as the lopped hornbeams in the Forest itself. Few of the girls were beauties by modern standards. Life in East London was too hard for that. But friendliness and good humour were universal—at least until drink got the better of the more hard-bitten. Grandparents were there too. The old ladies resplendent in feathered hats and voluminous skirts behind gay protective aprons, the old men wearing sober suits and either cloth caps or faded bowlers; but all with a knotted handkerchief round their necks.

By afternoon there would be as many as 13,000 people surging across the Plain, picnicking on the turf, screaming from the switchbacks, bestriding hobby horses or cockerels on the merry-go-rounds, trying their luck at coconut shies, or jogging along sedately on one of the many donkeys trotted out for the day. The younger adults, with their strong arms and wrists, would be giving impressive performances on the flying trapeze, which in the 1880s became a favourite at the Easter Fair. This flying trapeze consisted of a series of ropes with handles, or loops, to be grasped by the flyer as he or she swung round daringly from a ring attached to an upper rope. The flyers enjoyed the security of knowing that if they lost their hold they would fall into the rope net suspended below them; but the buxom girls thought chiefly of the moment when they would be caught in the arms of the strong youth waiting for them at the end of the flight, where the custom was to seize them and carry them screaming to a safe distance for a rough and tumble on the grass.

Strong-lunged showmen would bellow the claims of their respective sideshows, in which a pound might be won for a shilling or a glimpse obtained of dark secrets not to be disclosed in daylight. There might be a dancing bear or two, and for those who preferred milder pleasures there were the boats on Connaught Water to be hired for twopence a tour. But the most popular delights were those that provided the most jolts and the dizziest sense of motion. Then, as the day wore on, singing was started to soothe the nerves of those approaching exhaustion, and deaden the sound of the children, who by this time might be getting fractious. Such songs as "White wings that never grow weary", "Hi, tiddly i, tiddly i ti ti", or "Where did you get that 'at?" were among the most popular, the second being particularly appropriate as quite a few of the revellers were 'tiddly' by that time. Few except lovers ventured far into the woodland. Those who were not in a hurry to get their children home made their way to the Forest hostelries—the Royal Forest Hotel, the Royal Oak, the Robin Hood, the Wake Arms or the Owl at Sewardstone, where singing continued to strident pianos indoors or barrel organs in the forecourts. And so the revelry continued until the last penny was spent and the last ounce of energy exhausted.

Although Easter, Whitsuntide and August Bank Holidays were the most frenzied, most weekends were pretty hilarious long before the Corporation came into the picture. In giving evidence to a Select Committee on Royal Forests in April 1863, the Rev. Robert Boothby Heathcote, lord of the manor of Chingford Earls, said that no supervision was exercised over the

crowds that came out into the Forest every Sunday. Chingford
Plain was like a fairground most weekends, with knock-me-
downs, barrel organs, gipsy fortune-tellers and donkey drivers.
This was all taken for granted and he personally saw little
harm in it although it would be helpful to the residents if this
use could be confined to a small area round Queen Elizabeth's
Hunting Lodge at Chingford and the area in front of the
King's Oak at High Beach, which were the favourite places of
resort. There were 2,300 acres of forest in his manor and he
derived no income whatever from this particular use being
made of it; but he was perfectly happy to see people picnicking
under the trees, dancing on the green or capering about on
donkeys. Sometimes the donkey men got drunk and stray
animals had to be impounded. That was a nuisance, but it
wasn't worth making a fuss about. When asked how much
control he believed he had over the land, and whether he could
put a stop to the use the public were making of it, he said that
so far as he knew it was his land to do what he liked with. He
could enclose and develop it if he wished to do so. With this in
mind he had already constructed a road on which he intended
to build houses with a forest view. His long-term intention,
which he didn't expect to live long enough to achieve, was to
allocate a large area as permanent open space and build houses
round it. When asked if he didn't think the people who lived
in those houses would complain about the jollifications on the
green, his reply was: "Not more than they do now."

The Rev. Robert Boothby Heathcote could only speak for
Chingford Plain. At High Beach, Sir Charles Wake's agent was
less generous in his attitude; but then he hadn't grown up with
this reckless use of private property. Consequently, when asked,
he said that he was not aware of any "recreative rights" which
any man could have over another man's property. The
question was then put to him in specific terms. "Are you
aware," he was asked, "of the existence of a charter, dated in or
about the reign of Henry III, having reference to the use by the
citizens of London of portions of these forests?" His reply was
that he had heard of this for the first time the previous day, but
he understood that this applied only to Enfield Chase. He
knew of no such charter applying to Epping Forest.

The best evidence offered to this Select Committee came, as

might have been expected, from the one surviving Verderer, Col. George Palmer of Nazeing, who had been elected a Verderer in 1842 and claimed descent from a Palmer who had held the same office in the reign of Charles I. He was fully in favour of the traditional use of the Forest by the people of East London, although there were inevitably a few donkey men and gipsies of bad character who were referred to locally as the 'Forest Blacks'. Most of the people who came out were respectable artisans and tradesmen, and he saw no reason to try to exclude them so long as they behaved themselves. When asked if he believed these people had a legal right to use the Forest for their own recreation, he replied: "I think it is a prescriptive right, a right which they have exercised for eight hundred years past—from time immemorial."

"You never heard of any notice being put up on the Forest, warning people from trespassing, did you?" he was asked. "No," he replied, "but our officers have always warned people against lighting fires."

Pressed further, he recalled that there had been an occasion when Sir Charles Wake's agent, without Sir Charles's permission, had tried to compel the people who came out to High Beach to go to the public house for their refreshment. He had done this by destroying the springs and wells from which they got water to make tea. This had been a misguided attempt to promote the interests of the licensee, who was a tenant. When it had been brought to the notice of the Verderers by Sir George Cockburn of Woodredon, with "the full and entire sanction of Sir Charles Wake, who deprecated the acts of his servant", the Verderers had ordered the springs to be restored for the use of the public.

Still pressed to try to recollect any notice warning people off any part of the Forest, he reiterated that he did not remember ever seeing such a notice. But finally, in an effort to try to understand what the Committee were getting at, he conceded that such notices might have been put up by persons to whom the Commissioners of Woods and Forests had sold Crown rights, adding pointedly: "I think it is very likely and very possible that the persons who have purchased those rights assumed that they had purchased not only the Crown's rights, but the rights and privileges of everybody else."

To the clinching question: "Then, during the time that you have been a Verderer of the Forest, you have acknowledged the right of the public to resort to those places?" he replied with the one word: "Certainly."

Col. Palmer even held—and this may be surprising in days when the lords of Forest manors are so widely believed to have been a law unto themselves—that the Verderers had no right to turn anyone off the Forest for being drunk and disorderly, so long as they were not damaging the flora or fauna of the Forest. It was for the police, he said, to deal with disorderly behaviour. The duties of the Forest officers in this respect did not go beyond assisting the police, who brought the offenders before the magistrates in the normal manner. They were never brought before the Verderers' Courts. There can, however, have been few Verderers in those days who were not also magistrates, so it may have been immaterial which court they appeared before! Today, no Verderer who is also a magistrate would adjudicate in cases in which Forest offences are involved. In the nineteenth century they were probably less scrupulous.

In assessing the value of these attitudes of the well-to-do to high jinks in the Forest, it must be added that these were not confined to cockney artisans and tradespeople. Alderman Copeland of Walthamstow remembered being one of a party taking out twenty dozens of pigeons to release and shoot near Queen Elizabeth's Hunting Lodge. He agreed that most of the visitors came from the artisan class and remembered the days when it was a common sight to see families coming out in vans or on carts, pitching their tents in the Forest for the afternoon and unloading provisions for ample meals. There were old women living in Forest cottages who got their living by supplying hot water for tea.

Donkey rides were particularly popular with visitors to Epping Forest for many years. The donkeys lived well during the summer months, but when winter came and there were few visitors they were hired out to London market men who did not always treat them as well as they might have done. Gerald Buxton of Birch Hall, himself a Verderer and the son of Edward North Buxton, became concerned about their condition and started a donkey show, awarding a prize for every donkey without a sore place on it, prizes for the best animals, the best pair, the best train, and so on. They were judged by a vet, and the shows were popular events. The Keepers were in attendance in their velveteen coats and white breeches, and Keepers' Race was the highlight of the show. Each chose a donkey to ride in a race along a hundred-yard track with a ditch as handicap. The fun came when the donkey slithered down the ditch and threw the Keeper. Some of the older Keepers avoided this by riding briskly up the side of the ditch to where they knew they would find a log bridge to assist them across it. The other popular event at these donkey shows was the 'Ladies and Gentlemen's Race', in which the 'Quality' gave their workpeople and tenants the fun of seeing them come to grief. Up to the First World War donkeys could be bought in Northern Ireland for about thirty shillings apiece and brought over for sale to the London costermongers.

By the 1890s there could be as many as 100,000 to 200,000 people in the Forest on a Bank Holiday. As early as 1892 a letter was received signed by residents near Wanstead Flats asking for the fair held there on Bank Holiday to be either discontinued or curtailed. Their request was met by the Conservators to the extent of limiting the number of licences for swings, stalls, shows and so forth to fifty, and reducing the nuisance of noise by siting the fair as far from the houses as possible.

The residents in Wanstead and Woodford had good reason to be nervous for their safety while a fair was being held. We complain about violence and vandalism today, but both were just as prevalent in the nineteenth century, when gangs from Bethnal Green, Hoxton and Whitechapel would seek out rival gangs and beat them up with wooden truncheons weighted with pockets of lead if they were lucky enough to come upon them unarmed. Later, of course, the revenge of the gang taken by surprise would be equally violent. Skinheads, Hell's Angels, and the rest of them of the twentieth century were only the successors of similar gangs that have terrorized each succeeding generation. But the rapid increase in population along the southern borders of the Forest posed exceptional problems and special police had to be engaged for the duration of the Forest fairs. But although the population was in the south, the rowdiest events of the years continued to be on Chingford Plain, where it was not uncommon for Keepers to be beaten up while trying to quell disturbances among the drunks. Then, as now, windows were broken in railway carriages and fittings torn out as they have been by football crowds of a hundred years later. Then as now the boys had their girlfriends with them, and far from these being the civilizing influence they are sometimes supposed to be, it was commonly found that the louder the girls screamed the more belligerent the boys became.

The local courts had busy days following these fairs, and as the Chairman of the Bench was likely to be a Verderer, justice was not always unbiased, particularly when the boys were found to have done a bit of poaching to help them meet the day's expenses. But this did not always operate against the offender. There was the occasion when a poacher was brought before the justices at Epping with Gerald Buxton in the chair, charged with taking conies in the Forest. "But," exclaimed the Verderer chairman, "they might as well have all the rabbits there are. They are no good in the Forest!"

Chaffinch and goldfinch catchers were in a different category. For years they were the most detested of all the Forest visitors and with good reason. They came out from the East End to trap and snare birds for the London street markets. The usual method was to spread lime on sticks, which were then laid across branches. Below these either dummy birds or 'call' birds in cages were placed to attract the attention of those who had taken possession of the territory and thought it had been invaded. To give these 'call' birds the illusion of darkness their cages were covered with cloths. Sometimes the birds were cruelly blinded by a needle heated on a gas-ring. Another method of capture was to spread nets before bushes of sleeping birds. Lanterns were then swung behind the bushes and the birds awakened by shaking the branches. Fear of the light drove them instinctively into the nets. This wicked trade was stopped when Lord Buckmaster, supported by the N.S.P.C.A., got an Act passed prohibiting the sale of birds in small cages and the blinding of call birds.

A much more reputable way of earning a living in the

Forest was that of the charcoal burners, who gave character to it for many years. They spent the winter quietly collecting the dead wood lying on the Forest floor, then built great piles of it and covered each pile with turves until it took on the appearance of a wigwam. Long poles were laid in a circle round each pile to keep the turves in position. This was important, because each pile became an oven in which charcoal was slowly made. The heap was fired from the base and the greatest care had to be taken to ensure that the coverage remained complete and no flame was allowed to break through. If a glow appeared on the covering of the stack, earth was shovelled on to it immediately. Once started, the fire was allowed to smoulder on until it died out of its own accord. It was then allowed to cool and the charcoal was shovelled out. This was put into sacks and sold off at the Forest Superintendent's office.

Charcoal burning expanded as a result of so many new rides being made and so much underwood cut during the early years of Corporation management; but the conditions in which the charcoal burners lived in order to keep up their twenty-four hours' watch became a public scandal. They had neither fresh water nor decent sanitation. So in the spring of 1889 the Epping Forest Conservators had them housed.

Charcoal burning in Epping Forest died out in the closing years of the century, but was revived for a short time in 1908 at Cuckoo Pits, near Chingford, by two Loughton men, J. Cook and G. Bowtle. Charcoal stills were again to be found on the Forest in the early days of the 1939-45 war.

In nothing has the improvement in living standards since the turn of the century been seen to greater advantage than in the appearance of children visiting the Forest. Organized visits started in 1891. In May of that year an application was received from the secretary of the Ragged School Union for permission to erect a temporary structure in the Forest at Leytonstone to be used as a holiday resort and shelter for 'drift children' from the East End, the intention being to bring out parties of about 200 by train daily. By the end of the year it was estimated that over 10,000 had visited the Forest under this arrangement. The following summer the number increased to nearly 25,000.

This first centre was near the High Stone at Leytonstone. Later the most popular centre was in Staples Road, Loughton, after the Ragged School Union had changed its name to the Shaftesbury Society. Every day during the summer months right through to the Second World War scores and sometimes hundreds of children could be seen marching up Station Road and Forest Road, Loughton, eagerly expectant of a long day in the Forest. Few people today can imagine what this must have meant to them. Nor for that matter can most people appreciate how these children were viewed by some of the well-to-do residents of Loughton. Suffice it to say, that at one time their passing along the streets between the station and the Forest was thought to constitute such a threat to local health and hygiene that they were followed at a discreet distance by the Council's water-cart spraying disinfectant.

Gipsies were probably the most romantic frequenters of the Forest in those days. It is impossible to estimate their numbers over the entire area; but the Rev. John Whitaker Maitland took annual counts of them in his own parish and recorded the number in his parish register. In 1871 there were ninety-six in the total population of 2,439. Parsons were usually popular figures with gipsies, because they tended to be charitably disposed towards them. The gipsies found it useful to get their children baptised whatever their own religious beliefs were as a means of attracting charity from ladies in the congregation who saw them as brands to be plucked from the burning. Others saw them differently. Their fortune-telling activities were regarded as mischievous. They sometimes gained power over the feeble-minded, and they were always suspected of petty thieving and poaching. They would undoubtedly have settled in Epping Forest in even greater numbers if the Epping magistrates, who usually included at least one Verderer and all the lords of the Forest manors, did not regularly insist that the Keepers should move them on and even impound their beasts found grazing on the Forest, which was virtually their only effective weapon against them. This they were well able to do because the gipsies had no land qualification to give them rights of common, and consequently their animals were unmarked. So when the Conservators were able to put teeth into their system for controlling Epping Forest the gipsies tended to move across the River Roding into Hainault Forest.

Hainault Forest is outside the scope of this book, but it is interesting to find that when it came into the market and the Corporation considered buying it, Edward North Buxton, who was strongly in favour of the acquisition so that the ancient Forest of Waltham could be reconstituted, thought that it would be a much more attractive proposition if the gipsies could be got rid of. So he got permission to use the Epping Forest Keepers in an attempt to accomplish this. The gipsies, however, outwitted him. They refused to budge until he offered them thirty shillings for every tent or caravan they cleared. They took the money and departed. Thirty shillings was not often so easily come by in those days. But within a few weeks they were back bringing others with them!

But not all the converts so eagerly sought by the religious ladies of the more evangelical parishes were later to prove backsliders. There are only two memorials in Epping Forest. One is to Sir Winston Churchill, the other is to Gipsy Smith, who was born in a caravan under a hornbeam tree on Mill Plain, near the Napier Arms at Woodford. He attended a Methodist Sunday School at Walthamstow, where his teacher was Sir William Mallinson, chairman of the Beacontree Bench for many years and a generous local philanthropist. Gipsy Smith became a world-famous evangelist, and when he died on board the *Queen Mary* on his way to America in August 1947, Sir William Mallinson's son, Sir Stuart, asked the Conservators to give him permission to erect a memorial to the gipsy on Mill Plain. This was granted, although it was against the policy of the Conservators to allow such memorials, and in 1949 a block of Cornish granite was placed on the Plain inscribed:

> Gipsy Rodney Smith, M.B.E., who preached the Gospel to thousands on five Continents for seventy years, was born here March 31st, 1860, and called home journeying to America August 4th, 1947. "WHAT HATH GOD WROUGHT?"

Such, then, was the many-coloured coat that Epping Forest wore. Perhaps the last of the annual events that can be touched upon briefly here is evidence of the strength of its ancient sporting tradition. The Royal Hunt became the Lord Mayor's Hunt, which degenerated into a popular farce and had to be abolished. The City aldermen accepted this and hunted elsewhere. The local Masters of Hounds held on as long as they could in the Forest, the last being Henry Vigne, who hunted hares in the Forest from 1830 till his death at the age of eighty-seven in 1892. In 1903 an Epping Forest Harriers Club was formed on kennels being provided at Theydon Place, Epping, by John Gurney Pelly. But the cockney spirit persisted for a further twenty-two years. It expressed itself in the famous Cyclists' Meet. This assembled in Capel Road, Forest Gate, in the form of a procession of decorated bicycles organized by local cycling clubs to form tableaux of the kind more widely associated with torchlight processions. From Capel Road the route was along Centre Road and Blake Hall Road to Sir John Bethell's house at Wanstead, where the tableaux were judged while the grounds remained available. Later the judging was at the Eagle, Snaresbrook. From the Eagle the procession made its way to Woodford along the main road, sometimes taking refreshment at Guys Retreat, near the Roebuck Hotel at Buckhurst Hill, at other times leaving the High Road opposite the Horse and Well Hotel, to go down Whitehall Lane to Chingford and finally on to Riggs Retreat at High Beach for tea and a general jollification before returning by the same route. For the return journey in the dark the cycles were lit up by 'fairy' lights. Each year the costumes were changed, each club choosing its own. One year all the members of one club would be Scottish Highlanders, the next year Ancient Britons. Nautical subjects were always popular, the cyclists mounting their machines inside a model ship to which they harnessed themselves. The tableaux had individual cyclists in the club costume as outriders, and these would collect money *en route* for local hospitals. The last Meet was held on 20 August 1914. At the end of the war the motor car came into the ascendant and it would have been hopeless to attempt to revive the Meet.

One of the most fascinating phases in the social history of the Forest was its association with the short-lived vogue of refreshment 'Retreats', referred to above in connection with the Cyclists' Meet. Tea gardens had flourished for some time alongside Forest inns, either directly associated with them or at nearby cottages; but with the rapidly expanding population of late Victorian London, steadily improving communications and the opening up of the Forest by the Conservators, larger parties than ever before were coming out for pleasure and relaxation. The Great Eastern Railway contributed to the demand for refreshment houses by organizing day trips and cheap excursions to their newly built stations in the Forest towns. Horse-drawn wagonettes brought out Sunday School parties and groups of children organized by such bodies as the Shaftesbury Society and the Ragged School Union. Cottage gardens were too small for such parties; hostelries were associated in the minds of Sunday Schools and charitable societies with the 'Demon Drink'. The need was for commodious, simply furnished wooden structures in which large parties of all ages could sit down to inexpensive meals, with such ancillary amenities as swings, helter-skelters and roundabouts to keep the children amused for an hour or two.

The dominant figure in the 'Retreat' movement was John Riggs, who had begun his business life as a builder, but who seized on the new market with both enterprise and imagination by erecting huge pavilions in the most popular beauty spots and, on completing them, by going into business as 'catering contractor' specializing in non-alcoholic refreshment. He established his first 'Retreat' in 1879 in Brook Road, Buckhurst Hill, after failing to get planning permission for one opposite Queen Elizabeth's Hunting Lodge. But Riggs was not the first in the field. That distinction goes to Edward Bartholomew, of Fairmead Lodge near the old Fairmead Oak on the road to High Beach, who was catering for Sunday School parties as early as 1853. When members of the Common Council of the City of London, along with their friends and guests to the number of several hundreds, visited the Forest on a tour of inspection in October 1875, Fairmead Lodge was the only place of refreshment sufficiently well equipped to cater for them. The Bartholomew family continued to be associated with Forest catering for more than a hundred years.

John Riggs had a family of three sons and one daughter,

all of whom were drawn into the 'Retreat' business. William, who married a daughter of John Chilton of the Robin Hood public house, managed the Riggs Retreat at High Beach, which was opened in 1881. He claimed that he could provide teas for between 3,000 and 4,000 children at one time. Thomas managed the third Riggs Retreat at Coppice Row, Theydon Bois, opened by his father in 1883. The building stood until the Second World War, during which it was destroyed by a bomb. Of these and the many other 'Retreats' established in the Forest, not one remains. Many of them continued to cater for smaller parties until the 1950s; but they reached their peak immediately before the First World War. Between the two wars the motor car brought another social change, with its own problems as we shall see later. The beaches of Southend and Clacton came within easy reach of a new generation of pleasure-seekers. The Riggs family had anticipated the demands of a more mobile public by building 'Retreats' in the seaside resorts of Dovercourt, Clacton and Southend, and the days of Epping Forest as distinctively—and perhaps in a sense exclusively—the Cockney Paradise were over.*

*These notes on forest 'Retreats' are based on information collected by Bernard Ward.

CHAPTER IX

CONTROLLED RECREATION

THE EPPING FOREST ACT 1878 refers to "cricket and other sports", and empowers the Conservators to "lay out, form, and maintain cricket grounds and grounds for other sports, and, for the better use and enjoyment of the parts so set apart, to enter into agreements with, and confer special privileges on, particular clubs or schools". The Conservators are also empowered "to set apart and maintain bathing places, with the requisite shelter and conveniences".

Cricket had been played continuously on the Forest at Woodford since a club was founded there in 1735. The thirteen-a-side match played on the ground in July 1808 was the first cricket fixture ever played in Essex. In 1878 the Woodford Club had Edward North Buxton as president and was influentially supported. Its future was assured. The neighbouring club at Buckhurst Hill was no less fortunate. It was founded in 1864 and like the Woodford Club has always played on the Forest. Epping's relationship with the Forest has been less stable. A local club had a pitch on the Plain in 1850, but moved off in 1857. In the 'seventies the Cable brothers formed a club to play on Bell Common, their parents providing all the amenities. In 1896 the two Epping clubs amalgamated to play on a ground in Bury Lane, with a pavilion provided by the Cable brothers for which the vicar bore most of the cost. But the formation of the Essex Competition split the club about 1899, when the pitch on the Plain came back into use on ground that had been used for several years by the West Essex Polo Club. In 1947 the Epping Foresters' Cricket Club was formed to play on Mill Plain, adjoining Bell Common, and continues to play there at the time these pages are being written.

The first large-scale provision for games undertaken by the Conservators themselves was at Chingford, where on 26 July 1888 nineteen gentlemen met at the Royal Forest Hotel under the chairmanship of Edward North Buxton, and resolved to form a golf club to play on a course behind the hotel, on land placed at their disposal by the Conservators. The course was to be of nine holes, laid out by the Superintendent, Francis McKenzie, in consultation with two officials of the Royal Blackheath Club. Its immediate success was so great that in the following October permission was given for the nine holes to be extended to eighteen. Edward North Buxton, as chairman of the Club, was at the top of his form as a player. He had a handicap of One. He was further inspired by this response of the public to put the Club on the national as well as the local map. The Duke of Gloucester, as Ranger, was invited to become Patron. He graciously acceded, and shortly afterwards a communication was received from the Secretary of State advising that Her Majesty had graciously given permission for the Club to be called the Royal Epping Forest Golf Club. Again, Edward North Buxton was being true to the principle he always instilled into his family: "Be simple in your private lives, but splendid in your public ways!"

Despite the close association of the Club (with Edward North Buxton as chairman and Francis McKenzie as secretary) with the Forest, it remained an independent club until 1901, when the Corporation took over responsibility for maintaining the course. By this time the first flush of success had passed. Golf clubs had been established to play on Forest land at Epping and Woodford; the West Essex had come into competition. In 1888 the Royal Epping Forest had been the only golf club in Essex with open membership. Its only rival at that date was the club at Shoeburyness, for which membership was restricted to Royal Artillery officers and their friends. The position was very different in 1901. If the Corporation had not come to its rescue in that year with a scheme for public play on the same course, the Royal Epping Forest Club might well have been forced into liquidation. The Conservators now maintain their own club, with canteen and toilet facilities for the general public, and permit two other clubs to use the same course under Corporation control. This entails considerable expense to the Corporation, but is greatly appreciated by the players, who tend, however, to have reservations about the lack of respect shown to them by commoners' cattle.

Golf reached Epping in 1890, when an application was received by the Conservators for permission to play on the Plain. In the same year an application came from Woodford for a nine-hole course on 'The Lops'. The Epping club moved off the Forest; but a club was formed to play on a course on Forest land at Theydon Bois, which in 1968 was extended to eighteen holes. Both the Woodford Club and the Theydon Bois Club play by licence from the Conservators.

Football had been played on the Forest for a short time in 1859, when a few Old Harrovians founded the Forest Football Club to play on a ground behind the Royal Wanstead School, which was then known as the Infant Orphan Asylum, and later as the Royal Infant Orphanage. Its independent existence lasted only four years. In July 1890, however, the London Playing Fields Committee approached the Corporation with a proposal for developing Wanstead Flats and Chingford Plain by laying out a number of spaces for both cricket and football for the benefit of the general public. After discussion, an agreement was reached for laying out an area not exceeding twenty-five acres on the Flats and an area of similar size on Chingford Plain. These have been subject to various modifications over the years. At the present time eighteen acres are set apart at Chingford, where the local authority maintain the pitches. Wanstead has a different story, as will be seen from the following paragraph. With the exception of Chingford all other courses, pitches, grounds and so forth are held by licence and their conduct is the sole responsibility of the licensees.

The Wanstead Flats playing fields, which extend over an area of approximately 150 acres, became the vast enterprise it is today as the result of a scheme launched in 1952 by the Corporation in association with both the National, and the Essex County, Playing Fields Associations, supported by funds jointly furnished by the City Parochial Foundation, the Goldsmiths' Company, the Corporation of London and the Playing Fields Association. The Trust support was for a period of five years only. In 1957 a more permanent arrangement was made with the City Corporation whereby the Wanstead Flats Playing Fields Committee, which included representatives from the Conservators and from the Playing Fields Association, would undertake the running and management of the playing fields, while any excess of expenditure over income would be borne by the Corporation. This joint scheme for running the large area of these playing fields was negotiated with the City Corporation with the help of Sir Arthur Noble on behalf of the Playing Fields Association, which thus continued to play an active part in the development of the scheme. On 8 May 1958 an informal visit was made to the Flats by H.R.H. Prince Philip, Duke of Edinburgh, in his capacity as President of the National Playing Fields Association.

The value of the fields to East London amply repays all the work and money put into it. Approximately 8,000 school children and 100 clubs use the fields each week, the number varying according to the season, but amounting to upwards of a quarter of a million in any one year. These schools and clubs have the use of changing rooms built by the Corporation in stages between 1958 and 1968 with showers and all modern amenities. Since 1973 there have been sixty-two Association Football pitches, four hockey pitches and three Rugby Union pitches.

Provisions for bathing, which was mentioned in the Act, have been made by local authorities under conditions outside the range of Forest possibilities. Despite this, the Shoulder of Mutton Pond, Wanstead, has a long record of use by round-the-year enthusiasts, and the Wake Valley Pond continues to be used, although in diminishing numbers, by the hardy for regular bathing. Other ponds are used for the occasional dip; but the only large open-air swimming pool is in a disused gravel pit at Whipps Cross, and at the time of writing the future of this is uncertain.

The Whipps Cross Pool was constructed by the joint enterprise of the Leyton and Walthamstow Borough Councils, now incorporated in the London Borough of Waltham Forest. It can accommodate as many as 2,000 bathers; but the losses incurred in maintaining so large an open-air pool became prohibitive and the Council put up a scheme to the Conservators for modernizing the buildings as part of a recreational complex which would involve a considerable area of Forest land. As this would involve the Council in massive expenditure for the rebuilding of dressing-rooms and toilet blocks, together with the expansion of existing facilities by providing a paddling pool for children, a proposal for a restaurant on the site was included in the scheme as a means of securing an income. To anyone familiar with the terms of the Act, the difficulty of finding terms for allowing catering facilities that went so much beyond providing a service for people visiting the Forest specifically for recreation will be apparent. The Forest could so easily be drawn into use for parking the vehicles of persons visiting the restaurant for the sole purpose of having a meal. So the scheme could not be approved.

By far the most difficult recreational problem in Forest management has been that posed by horse-riders. In 1878 this hardly existed. In those pre-motoring days horse-riding was seen as a normal mode of travel and only marginally as recreational. Such riding as there was for pleasure was an individual or family form of exercise dispersed over the entire area of the Forest instead of being concentrated along tracks giving access to the woodland from commercially run riding schools. When riding schools first came into the picture, they were mainly concentrated in the south, where there were wide areas of grassland on relatively well-drained soil. Consequently, the damage to the Forest floor was insignificant and temporary, and the chief, if not the only, danger was to pedestrians startled by the sudden arrival of galloping horses. But during the 1930s these riding schools had so increased in number that complaints came in from the public so frequently that in 1937 the Conservators felt obliged to impose byelaw restrictions on riders in the area south of a line extending from Yardley Hill, Chingford, to Warren Hill, Loughton, by confining them to defined tracks.

Later, as the popularity of horse-riding for pleasure in-creased, and also, it has to be said, extended to riders with little knowledge of either animals or any sort of country code of behaviour, the much more vulnerable central areas of the Forest came to be affected, and the whole question of this particular use of the Forest had to be examined, involving, as it did, other legitimate users of its amenities. No other Forest pursuit affected others to anything like the same degree. The result of this examination was a policy decision that horse-riding should be recognized by the Conservators as a healthy exercise for which provision should be made, and the problem must be seen as one of containment. So money was spent on reinforcing popular tracks in the Hawksmouth and Warren Hill areas in the hope that riders would voluntarily keep to these and leave other parts to those who found their pleasures on foot. For several years these provisions proved adequate and the reinforcing of riding tracks became a regular part of the Forest programme of work.

Soon after the Second World War, however, building pressures in the south, with the consequent rise in the value of land, squeezed out the riding schools. These moved into the still rural northern parishes in which woodland predominated and where the old green rides afforded the only unobstructed routes. As the soil in this part of the Forest was heavy clay, these narrow tracks through dense thickets were quickly reduced to quagmires during the winter months, and rarely recovered during the short dry season of an English summer. The Conservators found themselves quite unable to keep pace with the increasing need for surfaced tracks to which riding might be confined, and as the green rides became impassable even to the riders themselves the nearby woodland was invaded until this also became unusable.

In 1961 the Conservators agreed to surface in depth certain lengths of rides that had become badly poached through excessive use in the hope of finding a more acceptable solution to the problem than the previous methods of reinforcement had provided. Five sections, running to a total length of 650 yards, were treated and the experiment appeared so successful that a costly programme was embarked upon for providing a network of riding tracks, with six to nine inches of hardcore surfaced with three inches of hoggin, accompanied by an improved system of drainage throughout the affected parts. In order to bring these tracks into full use it was also considered that it would be necessary to close parts of the Forest while the floor was allowed to recover.

While these plans were under discussion the riders them-selves got together, and in 1962 formed the Epping Forest

Riders Association. Considerable goodwill was shown on their part, and it is probably unfortunate that the Association was not formed earlier, because during the two previous years damage to the Forest floor had become so serious, and criticism of the Conservators so vocal, that the Committee felt obliged to examine the question of extending the restrictions of riding to defined tracks throughout the Forest: that is to say, imposing the restrictions that had been in operation since 1937 in the areas south of the line from Yardley Hill, Chingford, to Warren Hill, Loughton, to the areas north of it. This proposal seemed reasonable on paper, but doubts arose about its practicability. So the Superintendent was authorized to improve points of access to the woodland used by riders where pedestrians were inconvenienced, and to convene a meeting with horse riders with a view to gaining their co-operation. In the event, there were several meetings. At the original meeting at which the Epping Forest Association was formed, which was held at Wanstead on 23 July 1962, the problem had been outlined to the riders, who had expressed appreciation of what was being done to improve the surface of existing rides and tracks, and had agreed that if these could be extended sufficiently they would have the effect of drawing riders on to them and the nuisance would be abated. Later in the 'sixties it became clear that voluntary co-operation would not be sufficient.

By 1968 six or seven miles of gravel tracking had been laid in the central part of the Forest; but the date when the whole of the Forest could be covered was still remote and not everyone favoured the scheme. Meanwhile, conditions in the northern parts continued to deteriorate. The nature of the soil, the density of the woodland, the problems of drainage in certain parts between Epping and Loughton were such that these could never be treated as the parts to the south had been treated without ruining the entire character of these beautiful areas. More stringent regulations would have to be imposed during wet seasons. So again the riders were consulted with a view to getting some form of agreement to controls that would be flexible and exercised only as circumstances demanded. As an experiment, riding tracks were indicated not by notices as in the south, but by small boards strapped to trees, each board bearing a representation of the head and shoulders of a rider and the forequarters of a horse. By this means tracks could be quickly established and cancelled as ground conditions changed. These were not to be in place of gravel tracks, which would continue to be laid; but for use either where gravel tracks could not be laid or where this kind of posting might prove adequate for purposes of control. They were fully accepted by most of the riders as an alternative to banning horses from certain areas permanently.

Unhappily, not all riding schools were prepared to co-operate, and some riders became extremely militant in their attitude. As these establishments owed their very existence to the proximity of the Forest and their livelihood to the good-will of the Conservators, their attitude was difficult to understand by any reasonable person; but there it was, and they had to be regarded as constituting a menace from which other users of the Forest must be protected. So the Conservators reluctantly decided to seek parliamentary sanction for proposals designed to make reasonable provision for organized riding whilst at the same time safeguarding the interests of other Forest users. This proved more difficult than had been foreseen, even by those who had been wrestling with the problem for ten years or more. Basically, what was required was power to close any part of the Forest in the north for the limited period necessary to restore the Forest floor to a normal condition while the Conservators pressed on with their programme for twenty miles of gravel tracks. The complications, however, were immense, particularly having regard to the resistance that was likely to be expected from certain quarters, and the difficulty of enforcing byelaws that did not meet with reasonably general acceptance.

At this point, it was felt desirable to hold consultations on a much wider scale than formerly, and in 1968 the Eastern Sports Council was asked to examine and report on the problems arising from the conflict between the horse-riders and the other interests. Sir Arthur Noble, representing the Eastern Sports Council, gave valuable help by presiding over consultations with representatives of the Conservators, the British Horse Society, the Essex County Planning Department, the Standing Conference of Essex County Sports

Associations, and the Lea Valley Regional Park Authority in an endeavour to devise a scheme that would be just to all who had legitimate interests in the Forest. The British Horse Society maintained that riding was not at that time causing excessive damage and that the number of riders was not likely to increase in view of the apparent reluctance of planning departments to agree to new establishments. For the damage that was there for anyone to see they blamed that permanent begetter of all ills, the weather. With what degree of cynicism it is impossible to say, they submitted proposals for defined footpaths for pedestrians, which the riders would respect, and by this means remove one ground of complaint. They did not try to make out that pedestrians were doing any damage to the Forest floor, and made no helpful suggestions for meeting the needs of naturalists or many other legitimate users of the Forest who had at least as good a right as the riders had to roam the Forest at will, and who did no damage.

At the end of the consultations the Eastern Sports Council produced a carefully balanced report stating accurately and fairly what the points at issue were and expressing the opinion "that the increase of riding had caused an imbalance of use of the Forest for recreational purposes, and that some form of control must be introduced". This was generally accepted. The question was how far the control should go. The present position is that the City of London (Various Powers) Act 1971 permits the Conservators to prohibit the riding of horses in any part of the Forest if they consider it necessary to do so to protect the Forest floor or preserve the natural aspect, except along the special riding tracks designated for the purpose. In imposing these restrictions an undertaking was given to the Essex County Council that the all-weather rides would be extended to the length originally planned, as finances permitted.

CHAPTER X

GRAZING-RIGHT PROBLEMS

As WE HAVE SEEN, the Epping Forest Act 1878 provided that all rights of common pasture should continue as they existed when the Act was passed. These rights were attached to lands and tenements within the Forest parishes and were subject to a number of controls. The one requiring that the reeves should mark for every person that had the right of commoning "two cows for four pounds *per annum* rent or, in lieu of that scale of rental", any other scale of rental or annual value which appeared most advantageous to the commoners, has already been discussed. Any alterations in these rules and regulations required the consent of the Ranger, and must be subject to the overall control that they must not be inconsistent with the Act.

The ancient right of the parish vestries to nominate proper persons for appointment as reeves was to be preserved. Marking days were to be fixed, and unmarked beasts were to be impounded. All this was in accordance with long-established practice. Before the Act was passed, the last of the Verderers under the old regime, Col. Palmer, had given evidence that parish vestries had continued to nominate reeves even after Verderers' courts had fallen into abeyance.

But the twentieth century brought changes greater than ever before, and it became obvious that a system devised for a rural community needed modification to suit the needs of one that was becoming progressively urbanized. The difficulty about introducing such modification was that while the southern parishes were completely urbanized, those in the north remained rural. A further complication was that although the animals were turned out in the north, the best grass—or most of it—was in the south. Eventually it became

124

clear that the factor compelling action was the enormous increase in motorized traffic on Forest roads. The cattle were free to wander from one grazing ground to another, and when this involved crossing the busy London–Newmarket road the attendant screeching of brakes was evidence of the danger created. At the same time there were angry complaints about cattle invading gardens. So by the end of the 1950s the whole question of the continuance of grazing rights in any form was being widely discussed in the Forest parishes.

This was obviously a thorny subject for the Conservators, who knew that it was the existence of these very rights that saved Epping Forest for the public in the 1870s. However, in November 1959 the Epping Forest Committee invited the officers to prepare a report "on the rights of common on the Forest and their exercise and regulation, together with suggestions as to any amendments considered necessary or desirable to give effect to restrictions on grazing". The legal position was outlined in the reply. It was also pointed out that the presence of these animals was valuable in helping the Conservators to preserve the open aspect, in that without them areas that were now open would quickly revert to scrub. On the other side, it had to be recognized that the straying of these animals onto Forest roads was being increasingly criticized, and complaints from residents in streets bordering the Forest about the damage done by cattle invading their gardens were now numerous. It might be the position in law that the residents were at fault in not fencing off their gardens and keeping their gates shut; but the Conservators were anxious to keep their reputation as good neighbours. So to that end it was agreed that they should explore means of reducing to a minimum any inconvenience caused by the exercise of these ancient rights.

Much of the criticism arose from those who suffered from cattle making their way south to the great wedge of open waste lying within a solid block of terraced houses and small villas. By this time farming had ceased completely in the south, and most of the houses with large gardens had been pulled down to make way for smaller houses, which tended to be built without walled-in gardens. At the end of the discussions the Verderers were asked to meet the grazier commoners and sound them on the feasibility of:

1. Tethering horses on the Forest;
2. Keeping all untethered animals off the Forest between 21 December in any year and 24 March of the following year, both dates inclusive;
3. Providing a herdsman;
4. Adopting Chingford Lane, between Chingford Hatch and Woodford Green, as the southern boundary of the land over which untethered animals should be grazed;
5. Preparing a list of certain isolated areas in wholly rural surroundings, such as Epping Long Green, which should be free from these modifications in grazing rights.

If these concessions were acceptable to the grazier-commoners the Conservators would undertake to improve the quality of grass in the northern part of the Forest, and as an earnest of good faith equipment and material for implementing this part of the proposed agreement were immediately purchased, even though it was understood that the right which the commoners possessed of grazing over the wastes of Epping Forest did not require the Conservators to provide one single blade of grass, and that not one in twenty of those who possessed the right had any intention of exercising it.

It was recognized that any terms negotiated with the small minority of commoners turning out cattle would be no more than "a gentlemen's agreement", which could not be enforced against any of the commoners who were parties to it, and could not in any circumstances apply to the hundreds of commoners who were entitled to such rights but did not choose to exercise them. The commoners who turned out cattle agreed to try out the system, but for a variety of reasons it failed to work. Cattle continued to appear in the southern areas of the Forest, and when representations were made to the offending graziers they replied that they had been compelled to allow their cattle to graze the southern areas during a period of exceptionally warm weather, which had caused the grassland in the north to become inadequate. At the same time they reiterated their firm intention to abide by their agreement so long as the grassland improvement promised by the Conservators gave them sufficient feed to offset the loss of the grazing land in the south. They did keep their promise to take their cattle off the Forest altogether between 21 December and 24 March for several years, but the weakness of that part of the bargain was that November frequently brought fogs, and when that happened it was difficult to locate the cattle until angry residents complained of the damage that had been done by the cattle they had actually found lying peacefully on their lawns!

It was small comfort to these angry residents to be told that the Corporation had no responsibility for the protection of private property bordering the Forest, and that far from having any obligation to restrict the rights of commoning in the interests of local residents, they had not even power to make rules to control the use the commoners' cattle made of highways running through the Forest. Public feeling was such that it looked at though the Conservators would have to face the question they had so far tried to evade, namely, whether circumstances had so changed since the Act was passed that it had become reasonable to seek parliamentary sanction for imposing limits on the right of commoning in Epping Forest. To anyone familiar with the terms of the Act this was seen as being so revolutionary an amendment that it was felt that yet another attempt must be made to try to get the grievances dealt with by encouraging the commoners to make one more effort to make the system of containment work, pointing out that the improvement of the grazing was as great a voluntary contribution on the part of the Conservators to the solution of the problems as the limitation of use was on the part of the grazier-commoners.

The Conservators left no one in any doubt about the effort they were prepared to make. Thirty acres of Whitehall Plain and Birkbeck were treated; one hundred acres of Chingford Plain, thirty-five acres at Hawksmouth and Yardley Hill, ninety acres at Fairmead Bottom and Almshouse Plain, and thirty acres of Honey Lane Quarters as well as several smaller areas were all fertilized and made to yield good crops of grass in the parts of the Forest most convenient for the graziers, who all lived in the north-west. But despite these efforts on the part of the Conservators, in the spring of 1960 the graziers

met the Verderers and the Superintendent and said that they
had been unable to keep their part of the bargain. The cattle
could not be held north of the agreed line. Having said this,
they went on to refer to a meeting promoted by Walthamstow Borough Council at which the abolition of grazing
rights was discussed, and asked what sort of compensation
they might expect if this proposal were pursued. They were
pessimistic about being able to hold out indefinitely against
social pressures in favour of the abolition of grazing on the
Forest, and as businessmen they wanted to know what sort of
price they might expect if they were bought out.

The Corporation then faced the complicated legal issue
involved. Those turning out were not the only commoners
enjoying such rights. It was conceivable, if highly improbable,
that the eight or ten then exercising these rights might be
bought out and another eight or ten then decide to exercise
rights, and so on until several hundred commoners had
gained awards for the loss of rights they had never had the
slightest intention of exercising. Nor was it certain that the
people living in the northern parts would want to see the
cattle taken off the Forest. The Members of Parliament for
the Forest constituencies might not speak with one voice
when the question came before Parliament. The Conservators
themselves were all too well aware of the problem they
would have in preserving open spaces for the enjoyment of
the public if the cattle were taken off. Artificial means of
achieving this would have to be introduced, and experiments
were actually made with the use of a chain flail which would
cut the grass in a rough manner and prevent any of the
existing open spaces taking on the appearance of mown lawns.
Even this was very different from the appearance achieved by
the close cropping by cattle, and it did nothing to consolidate
the turf. At the end of that same year (1960) the commoners
with whom the agreement had been made announced that
they had made no plans to remove their cattle that winter,
and the Conservators must no longer assume that the voluntary concessions made in the past would be repeated.

It was in these circumstances that the Corporation finally
decided in July 1961 that Parliament must be invited to
determine whether the time had come for the Act to be

24 & 25. Riggs Retreat, Wellington Hill, High Beach

26 & 27. Riggs Retreat, Wellington Hill, High Beach

28. John Riggs and family

29. William Riggs and daughter 'Billie'

30. Mrs Dorothy Fairfax (Miss Billie Riggs)

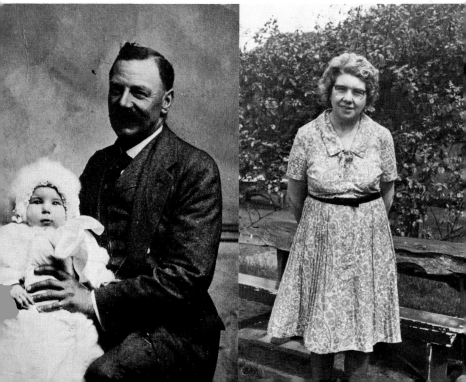

31 & 32. Wanstead Park

33. Wanstead Park

34. 'Princely Piety, or the Worshippers at Wanstead'.
A coloured engraving by G. Cruickshank from the
Scourge, December 1811. In the centre is Catherine
Tylney Long and on her left is the Duke of Clarence
and Mrs Jordan. Clarence is pushing back Baron de
Geramb who is menaced by Napoleon. On the other
side is Sir Lumley Skeffington with a quizzing glass, and
next to him Mr Romeo Coates. The two men fighting
are Mr Wellesley Pole and Lord Kilworth

35. Sidney Butt, Forest Keeper (1894-1937)

36. Forest Keepers *circa* 1878. Left to right they are: Chas. Watkins, J. Chellis (Head Keeper), H. Butt, Jas. Pearce, J. Dunning, Fredk. Luffman (Head Keeper) and Wm. D'Oyley (Superintendent).

37. Forest Keepers 1974. Left to right they are: A. Holland, E. Weedon and D. Cheatle

38.   Forest Keeper Chas. Watkins   39.   Forest Keeper John Little

40.   The Warren, the Forest Superintendent's residence

amended; not to abolish grazing, but to regulate it by requiring that all animals turned out should be tethered. It would obviously not be possible to tether large herds of cattle; but Parliament might well take the view that the object of preserving commoners' rights as set out in the Act of 1878 was, not to enable cattle dealers to exploit the cheap grazing available on the Forest wastes, but to enable smallholders to supplement their meagre incomes by turning out the odd beast or two. If Parliament did take that view, tethering might be thought to be more consistent with the spirit of the Act than the large-scale turning out by a few graziers that had succeeded it. And even if the issue did not turn on so narrow a question as this, it seemed to the Conservators that the social environment of the Forest had changed so radically since the Act was passed that Parliament might like to express its view on the relevance of its terms in the 1960s. If, however, Parliament decided that the Act should remain unamended in this way, the Conservators would have their answer both to the present critics and to any that might come forward as a result of the Royal Commission's Report. They would also continue to have the cattle to keep down the scrub, and in all their thinking this was a major consideration.

The Corporation's proposals for abating nuisances by restricting the movement of cattle were placed before Parliament in a City of London (Various Powers) Bill, which was given an unopposed Second Reading on 3 April 1962, but suffered emasculation at Committee stage. Neither the Committee nor any witness appearing before it seriously questioned that the presence of cattle on busy roads was at all times a nuisance and could be a danger. Doubts on the effectiveness of the remedies proposed turned on their practicability. Mr John Harvey, Member for Walthamstow East and now a Verderer, in moving that the Bill be recommitted, pointed out that the Corporation was itself restricted in the remedies it could suggest. As the champion of the commoners in the fight to preserve the freedom of the Forest in the 1870s it would ill become it to ask Parliament to abolish commoners' rights ninety years later. The powers being sought had the object of preserving the rights of common as they were known in the

1870s, which were very different from the current method of grazing beef cattle. The right of the active commoners to adjust their grazing practice to modern conditions was fully recognized, and the Corporation had expressed willingness to compensate them for any diminution in their rights. In the event, the number of Preservation Societies opposing the Bill proved too strong and the Corporation did not receive the powers it sought.

In view of the fight there was in those early years over entitlement to commoners' rights, it may be thought odd that the ancient scale of qualification should so long have remained unchanged. Even now nothing has been done to revalue the two cows for £4 rental rule. The only reasonable reassessment would be on acreage, but this would be accepting a principle of entitlement entirely different from that of cottager-need. There is, however, no point in seeking a different scale of entitlement, because the Forest is now undergrazed and scores of well-established farmers would not for one moment consider turning out their valuable animals to roam at will today. This puts the grazier-commoners who do turn out into a highly privileged position, having regard to the fact that they are such a small minority of the Epping Forest commoners who once every seven years themselves turn out to vote for the Verderers. The size of the support they can command from their fellow commoners was made plain when they put up a nominee of their own for the 1971 election. As the Conservators have always recognized the value of having cattle on the Forest, the Epping Forest Committee—the Verderers especially—have at all times been ready to co-operate with the grazier-commoners in finding solutions to the problems arising from straying cattle. The graziers have frequently failed to appreciate that the Conservators are under no obligation to provide either services or fodder. In view of the attitude adopted by some of the grazier-commoners during recent years the Epping Forest Committee has given serious thought to turning out a herd of its own. This herd could be folded over a succession of areas as required, and as visualized in suggestions put forward by the Waltham Forest Trades Council. Only a light fence would be required for this, and it is probable that if the scheme were adopted, round-the-clock supervision would be given. On the other hand, if the scheme were adopted the Conservators might incur liability for damage done by their animals.

When the winter of 1974 brought another crop of complaints about straying cattle entering gardens and doing hundreds of pounds worth of damage, the Committee, at its January meeting in 1975, recommended that the Corporation should seek power to establish a close season for grazing from 15 November in one year until 15 April in the following year.

CHAPTER XI

PRESERVING THE NATURAL ASPECT IN THE TWENTIETH CENTURY

WHETHER the state of advanced decay in which the Conservators found the Forest in 1878 was natural or unnatural, it was not a condition to be preserved. So it was necessary to decide what "the natural aspect", as applied to Epping Forest, meant. Fortunately, Edward North Buxton rose to the challenge and laid down principles that in his opinion should be followed consistently at all times. He set them out under four heads: variety of scenery, preservation of natural features, restoration of the natural aspect where this had been lost, and regeneration.

From the beginning of its recorded history Epping Forest has been remarkable for exhibiting an unusual variety of soil conditions for so small an area, and consequently of flora and fauna. To explain this one has to go back to the end of the Ice Age, when the great ice sheet that slid down eastern England split on the high bank of the Roothings to the north of the Forest, one lobe scouring out what became the Lea Valley, the other what became the Roding Valley, and as it moved forward like two outstretched arms, squeezing the soil between into the rugged contours of Epping Forest, which are so different from those of either the gently undulating country-side to the north or the plain to the south.

This broken, uneven terrain proved so unworkable by the Saxons, who settled along the river banks, that when the Normans came its advantages for pleasure were immediately apparent and it was preserved for the Sovereign's sport. Later, the successive owners of the soil along the river borders added their own contributions to this inherent variety by the uses to which they put their manors. These tended to be more individualized than those in other parts of the country as a result of poor communications both east–west and north–south. Broadly speaking, open spaces had been extended and brought under cultivation in the south and west, while the dense woodland in the centre tended to thin out towards the north and north-east, where, although the land was hilly it was not rugged, and the influence of Waltham Abbey had brought granges for the monks and imparked enclosures for court favourites in such places as Birch Hall at Theydon Bois, Hill Hall at Theydon Mount, Gaynes Park at Theydon Garnon and, on the west, Holy Field at Waltham Abbey.

In the vicinity of Epping, the Lower Forest and Bell Common continued to be grazed over a long period. Bell Common was the last grazing ground for cattle being driven down from the eastern marshes to the great marts near London, and the Bell Inn itself was known as the drovers' inn. While Epping remained the first main staging post out of London on the Newmarket road its inns stabled as many as 200 horses. These would be turned out each evening and headed towards the Lower Forest to the north, where they would graze contentedly and lie out all night until brought in for changes the following day. With the end of the coaching trade much of this grazing land must have reverted to scrub, from which it has never been rescued, and this might well be thought an area in which Edward North Buxton's idea of restoring, if not the natural (whatever that may mean) at least the traditional aspect might be kept in mind. The siting of the old water trough, now no longer there, at the junction of the Chelmsford road with the Newmarket road, was long a reminder of those pastoral days. It is in the Lower Forest also that we have clear evidence of different soil conditions in the presence of ash trees, rare in other parts. Oaks also flourish there.

In contrast, the Forest to the south of Epping runs along a ridge with natural drainage provided by valleys running down from Epping Thicks towards Theydon Bois, producing fine beeches and many unpollarded hornbeams, which are so different from those nearer Loughton. Theydon High Wood has beeches resembling those in a continental Forest, whilst nearer Birch Hall the trees on Oak Hill are all of approximately the same age, the result of a planting following a clearing made by the former lord of the manor who planned to build himself a house there. Many of the trees on the Theydon side of the valley running down from the Newmarket road are of comparatively recent growth. They are on land cleared during the nineteenth century.

A limited amount of planting was undertaken in the north of the Forest by the Conservators soon after taking over. Belts of trees were planted specifically to screen new buildings from Forest users, an excuse not always appreciated by those who lived in the buildings. Even now, when purchasers of new houses complain that their view into the Forest is obstructed by the growth of scrub and the branches of trees along the Forest verge, they have to be told as tactfully as possible that it is no part of the duty of the Conservators to ensure that local residents enjoy the maximum .advantage of living so near the Forest, but that it may be their duty to ensure that people resorting to the Forest from other places shall not have their enjoyment of the rural environment spoiled by the sight of belts of urban development. It is true, however, that some of this screening growth has now become a nuisance for other reasons and has to be cut back. It attracts, for example, litter, and may afford cover to drivers using the Forest for improper purposes.

Overhanging growth where houses are built on the edge of the Forest is a constant anxiety because it may entail legal liability. In the nineteenth century most of the houses on the Forest verge had large gardens. Now these gardens are split up as the price of land rises and smaller houses are built much too close to Forest trees. When purchased in spring or summer the advantage of looking out into woodland is very pleasant, but when winter comes the falling leaves are regarded as an intolerable nuisance, and if roots appear through the garage floor angry protests come in to the Superintendent's office. Now that the Forest in the southern parishes is almost entirely enclosed by houses, the wood gang could spend all their time cutting back branches to meet these complaints. Trees overhanging highways are a more serious matter. These are surveyed regularly and any that might be thought to constitute a hazard are ruthlessly cut back or felled.

For many years Epping Forest Keepers were recruited from time-expired servicemen from the Armed Forces; but in course of time these sources became less productive than they had been—largely, no doubt, because the hours of work and terms of service were less attractive than those in many jobs available on pension; but the job itself continues to have great attraction for the right men, and the average length of service of Forest Keepers and other employees of the Corporation must be the envy of many employers of labour.

For the important business of tree thinning a woodgang of twelve to eighteen is employed under a foreman to carry out the instructions of the Conservators. Each year summer and winter programmes of work in the Forest in keeping with the pattern started in those early years are discussed by the Superintendent with the Verderers and the chairman of the Epping Forest Committee. Their advice is then tendered to the full committee, which visits the Forest each Saturday before the second Monday of the month throughout the year with the exception of the four winter months, to see what is proposed, consider representations from the public on the spot and reach decisions. From time to time representatives of local authorities, Members of Parliament for the Forest constituencies, forestry bodies, conservationists from other parts of the country and other interested parties are invited to join the committee for these monthly inspections of the Forest, which follow a time-honoured pattern fully consistent with the best traditions of democratic consultation and, incidentally, of City hospitality.

Certain matters tend to be permanent parts of the agenda for these visits—subject, happily, to seasonal variation to relieve the monotony. Apart from the perennial complaints about straying cattle or the damage done by horse-riders, there are the regular complaints about overhanging growth, thistles shedding seeds that are blown by the wind into neat suburban gardens, stagnant ponds, the spread of scrub into grassland, and so forth. Thinning near frequented parts always produces a crop of protests. Many of these come from residents who have known the Forest all their lives and must know that, far from reducing the area of woodland, the Conservators are fighting a losing battle against its expansion.

Fortunately, there are a great number of friends of the Forest who appreciate what is being done to preserve the natural aspect and from time to time offer valuable suggestions for improvement. It is noticeable that much of the criticism during the 'seventies is of too little clearance of scrub. It rather looks as if the clearance made in the first years of Corporation management was so drastic that clearings made then remained open for fifty years or more. Certainly the spread of scrub during the past thirty years has been marked, and it does look as if a concerted attack will have to be made on it. To name only a few of the places where parts of the Forest that were open thirty years ago are now rapidly reverting to scrub, even where commonly used, there are Wanstead Flats, Copt Hall Green, Baldwins Hill, Strawberry Hill, Yardley Hill, Bell Common, the Plain, and the Rifle Range at Woodredon Hill. This natural evolution towards a woodland state is proceeding at an accelerating rate in all these places, and while this has been going on birch trees have invaded heathland; yet thinning now removes approximately 1,000 tons of timber annually. Incidentally, although this yields a small income, it is never forgotten that the Forest is run for amenity, and the profit from any project is never the determining consideration.

During the 1970s the Conservators have had another problem on their hands in the arrival of Dutch elm disease. This struck the Forest in 1971. During that year 2,000 trees had to be felled; in 1972 4,000 and in 1973 5,000. The disease continued to be virulent, and at the time of writing the total loss is 15,000 trees. Their removal greatly reduced the availability of woodmen for clearing thorn and scrub undergrowth.

Vigorous growth, however, is not universal on the Forest. In 1955 the Conservators became concerned that over a large area little new growth was to be seen even where the trees had been thinned to admit light and rain. This was particularly apparent in the beech woods at High Beach. To break up the soil, a disc plough was brought into use with fair results. The dense canopy of the beeches and demands they made on the soil suggested that certain areas were sick of producing beech and required more vigorous thinning to start a new cycle. It was in this same year that, on 25 September, the oldest and best-known tree in the Forest, the Fairmead Oak, was destroyed by fire. In the Leyton Hills soil erosion and the lowering of the water table is seriously affecting regeneration.

In general, however, it may be said that in the early years of management the Conservators fought to save the woodland from the depredation of loppers and deer stealers; now they fight resurgent Nature to prevent large areas of the Forest becoming inaccessible. By means as natural as can be achieved they aim to preserve the characteristic variety of the Forest woodland so that every legitimate interest in natural history can be cultivated and catered for, and to provide a rotation of growth so that trees of all ages can be seen and enjoyed by visitors. When a City alderman, visiting the Forest on one of the monthly inspections, had this explained to him, he said: "Well, yes, I follow that; but surely the test of whether you are on right lines or not is whether you achieve the desired results. Where can we see the end-product?" As the whole process is so long term and experimental, and everything done is subject to natural forces that are unpredictable, it was perhaps understandable that the alderman received from the Superintendent the reply: "In Heaven, sir."

At all events, if the Conservators were seeking perfection as the orderly-minded townsman sees it, they would not be preserving the natural aspect of so large a Forest, because although Epping Forest is small by comparison with the New Forest, it has 3,000 acres in one block between Epping and Woodford, which may well be the largest area of mixed beech, oak and hornbeam in England.

In making plans for summer or winter programmes of work the Conservators always have to bear in mind that special circumstances may intervene.

> The best laid plans o' mice and men
> Gang aft agley.

The incidence of the Dutch elm disease was one example. A succession of exceptionally dry summers in the 1970s has been another. Much of the work in the Forest is too varied to be dealt with in detail here. There is, for example, the continuous work of keeping Forest pests under control. Rabbits were a menace at one time, jays may be too numerous at another. For many years jay shoots were popular annual events for members of the Forest Committee and their friends. The Verderers placed the guns and the Keepers acted as beaters, striking the trees along the path of the drive. The main disturbing element was provided by the veteran Keeper Butt who carried a wooden rattle, the sound of which was sufficient to put up all the birds, causing them to flit from tree to tree until they reached the line of the guns. These annual shoots were stopped during the long and memorable chairmanship of the Committee by Samuel Sheppard, who disliked intensely the thought of anything so beautiful being shot for sport. Forest pests, however, have to be destroyed, and the Warrener rids the area of hundreds of pigeons, rabbits and rats annually.

Grey squirrels have been another pest. During the second half of 1972, 886 were shot by Keepers. Older people still remember the attractive red squirrel being common. They were still to be seen in 1956 in the area between the Wake Arms and Theydon Bois. A number were seen the same year in the vicinity of Sandpit Plain and Blackweir Hill. Keeper Holland reported seeing numbers of between twenty-eight and forty-three on different dates in 1956. They were still common on Sandpit Plain in 1957.

Perhaps the biggest factor making for change in the natural aspect of the Forest has been in the number of cattle enlarged; but visitors, too, have changed their habits. There are more horse-riders now. There are also more visitors coming by car. These remain near the car parks. But to the Forest lover the most interesting changes are the natural ones that mere man may find difficult to explain. Beeches seem to have come in great numbers during the nineteenth century. To some Forest lovers the most noticeable feature during the last thirty years has been the rapid increase in the number of oaks, which had been sparse since the massive clearance for the Navy during the second half of the seventeenth century and the first quarter of the eighteenth.

As local men, the Verderers are well placed to observe these changes and to be able to work with Nature, not against it.

In conclusion this might be a fitting place to pay tribute to the outstanding contribution of the Buxton family in guiding the destinies of Epping Forest in the field. With the death of the second Edward North Buxton in 1957 came the first break in the family association with the office of Verderer since 1878. The first Edward North Buxton served as Verderer for forty-four years, Sir Thomas Fowell Buxton for twenty-four; Gerald Buxton, the son of the first Edward North, for twenty-two years, the second Edward North (son of Gerald and grandson of the first Edward North) for thirty-three years—an average of thirty-one years, and during much of the time they were in double harness as Verderers. They were much more than local landowners. The second Edward North Buxton got a double-first in the Natural Science Tripos and a diploma in Forestry at Trinity College, Cambridge. He served throughout the Second World War on top secret work in the map room of the Cabinet War Office. He was chairman of the Commons Open Spaces and Foot-paths Preservation Society, on the Council of the Nature Conservancy, on the executive council of the National Trust, and he served on the Hobhouse Committee on National Parks. In all these he was following the tradition of a family that had probably done more than any other to formulate the policies of these bodies, which gave him the unique advantage in discussions of not only knowing the law regarding any question relating to Nature Conservation that came up—and he always had this at his finger-tips—but what was so much more helpful, of being able to explain how and why the law came to be formulated in the way it was.

The Buxton Verderers were always sensitive to the need to readjust from time to time the balance between the provision of facilities for recreation and the preservation of the natural aspect. With the progressive urbanization of the region, and the establishment of the Lea Valley Park for organized recreation, it seems reasonable to believe that these great pioneers would now see the need to safeguard the natural aspect as paramount.

CHAPTER XII

THE FOREST DEER

THE BLACK FALLOW DEER of Epping Forest are smaller than park deer and their antlers less branched. Although mole-coloured rather than black, toning down to a greyish brown on the neck and underparts, they are so dark that the mottles which are so conspicuous a feature in the coats of park fallow are only visible on close examination after death. The origin of this wild black species remains in doubt. They have been said to be the oldest fallow deer in Britain, and their intro-duction has been attributed to the Phoenicians, the Romans, the Danes, the Normans and even the Stuarts. Edward North Buxton in the later editions of his guide to Epping Forest says of them: "They have wandered there for many centuries, but are believed not to be indigenous, but to have been intro-duced by the Danes." In the first edition he had attributed their introduction to the Romans. We may take it that he had consulted the most reputable authorities of his day and that they were in doubt. Today we may go further with the doubt and say that there is no reliable evidence anywhere for saying either where they came from or whether they had to be introduced by anyone. They may already have been here when the first invaders arrived. What is not in doubt is that the Epping Forest deer are the last survivors of the herds that roamed the country before deer parks were thought of.

Ever since the Norman Conquest, fallow deer have been imported to restock the royal parks and forests. It has been stated that James I first imported the black variety from Norway for this purpose; but we know that there were black fallow deer in English parks before his time. They were recorded in Windsor Park in 1465. The last two herds to be found in private parks in England were those at Packington

Park, near Coventry, and at Levens Park, Westmorland. As Packington was imparked by Sir Clement Fisher in the reign of James I, the history of the herd cannot be traced before that date, and the Levens Park herd is believed to be descended from deer introduced about 1590 from Norway. As there is no documentary evidence for this it is a tradition that must be treated with the reserve with which all local traditions should be treated.

Whatever the origin of the Epping Forest herd, it was down to twelve does and one buck when the Conservators were charged to preserve the herd "as objects of ornament in the Forest". It is this clause that gives the Corporation responsibility for the herd. As the deer were wild and the Forest unenclosed in 1878 nobody could establish ownership at that date. It is doubtful whether anybody in 1878 would have wished to do so. The Epping Forest deer would then be judged inferior to park deer and classed as vermin. In the 1870s there were ten deer parks in Essex, with a total of approximately 1,500 fallow deer between them. An invasion by Epping deer would be looked upon with as much disfavour in those days as the appearance of park deer in the Forest is by the Conservators today.

In the days of the royal forest the most valued deer had been the red. These were viewed with increasing disfavour by neighbouring farmers and landowners until the last of them were removed to Windsor Forest by William IV early in the nineteenth century. The fallow had multiplied during the eighteenth century; but great numbers of them had been killed by the navvies who worked on the construction of the Epping New Road in the 1830s. Their method had been to occupy a barn on Fairmead with holes bored in the side, strew feed round the barn, and shoot off the deer that took advantage of it. So great was the destruction that the herd would have disappeared altogether if it had not been for the intervention of the Rev. John Whitaker Maitland, who took a great interest in the wild life of the Forest during the years immediately preceding its acquisition by the Corporation of London.

The other species once found in the Forest, the roe, were introduced by Edward North Buxton in February 1884, when he bought two bucks and four does from Mr Mansell Pleydell and Mr Charles Hambro, who had estates in the Vale of Blackmore in Dorset. The roe, however, colonized only small areas, most notably Great and Little Monkwood and the valley between these woods and the Epping road, a small area west and north of Loughton Camp, and another small area near the Cuckoo Pits, west of Fairmead. At the same time some of them left the Forest to colonize Copped Hall woodlands.

In September 1884 one stag and two hinds of red deer were returned to the Forest from Windsor, so that at the end of that year there were three varieties of deer to be found in Epping Forest.

The reintroduction of red deer proved a mistake. The following March landowners and farmers in the Waltham Abbey district complained bitterly about the amount of damage they were doing, and once again they had to be removed. The roe never settled. They died off of their own accord, the last record of them being made by Edward North Buxton during the 1970s. The most probable reason for this is lack of the dense cover they favour and the freedom from disturbance essential to them. If the roe had remained we might have had more information about the Forest deer than we have so far obtained with only the fallow, with their greater mobility, to observe. Major Anthony Buxton, son of the first Edward North, wrote interestingly about his recollections of the roe deer in Epping Forest in *Country Life,* 17 December 1948, particularly about their mating habits, and again in the issue of 23 February 1951. The roe deer on heat is a coquettish creature, who so excites the male with her antics that he loses his normal fear. Major Buxton tells us that he saw a roe buck serve a doe ten times in half an hour.

The chestnut-brown muntjac, a small Asiatic deer no bigger than a large dog, turns up in the Forest occasionally. One was seen by Keeper Holland near Copped Hall in February 1959, another was found dead on the Epping road at Buckhurst Hill in March 1973. They had probably strayed from a private park near Broxbourne, or possibly from either Whipsnade Zoo or Woburn.

The greatest excitement occurs when a white buck appears

among the fallow does. At one time romantic ladies had a
passion for white does. Several parks had all-white herds. In
Epping Forest the appearance of a white fawn of either sex
has always been attended by superstition, and although the
only way to maintain colour uniformity is to shoot off any
animal of another colour, it is action that invariably produces
alarm. Despite this, in 1950 the Conservators became so concerned by the obvious results of having had a cream-coloured
buck at large during the two previous breeding seasons that
they decided to eliminate him before the next breeding season
came around. Another 'white' buck roamed the Forest for
several years in the late 'fifties; but was found dead at Woodredon by Keeper Biggs on 28 October 1960. He was then
judged to be about eight years old and the yellow in his coat,
which gave him the cream-coloured, or dirty-white, appearance, was seen to be due to the presence of red hairs.

Fallow deer cast their antlers at the end of April, the older
bucks casting them first. The new head takes four months to
grow and harden off. In September, when the antlers are
clean, bucks may be seen rubbing them against trees, prefer-
ring for the purpose a dead bough rather than one with sap
in it. So long as the pedicle is undamaged an antler broken off
one year is replaced by a perfect one the following year. A
fallow buck reaches maturity at six, remains in his prime
until eight or nine, and after that declines rapidly. Few reach
the age of fourteen. The does start breeding at two and drop
their fawns in bracken in July. When about one week old
these follow their mothers out into the open and may be seen
grouped under a tree. The fear of humans comes early but
does not appear to be innate. A former Verderer, Bernard
Cook, used to relate how a very young fawn was seen trot-
ting at the side of a small girl in the Forest, showing no sign
of fear until the parent doe leapt out of the brushwood and
instantaneously communicated her own fear to the fawn. At
the height of the rut the bucks seldom feed, but they require
water. At the start of the season they take possession of their
chosen territory, in which the does seek them out, or so it
appears, each buck welcoming as many does as care to join
him. The relationship appears to be casual. The bucks show
little possessive instinct towards their does. If one leaves for

another buck the first shows no concern. She, however, may soon find herself in trouble with her new buck. Does are occasionally found killed or mutilated. The most probable explanation of this seems to be that the does drift into the new harem while still in season, which means that they avoid the attentions of the new buck; but although unwilling to stand for him, the newly arrived doe is still in a condition to excite the buck's desires, and this provokes him into knocking her about. This interpretation of what happens may be thought speculative, and it is conceded that evasive behaviour is normal on the part of the does—as indeed of females generally—and the bucks enjoy their playing 'hard to get'. Like human beings, however, the bucks have their breaking point and a flirtatious doe may find that she has taunted her buck beyond his power of endurance and she must take the consequences.

The rut reaches its height about 25 October, just at the time when the autumn colours are at their richest. The air at this time becomes crisp as the autumn winds blow in from the east and the entire Forest reaches a climax of fulfilment. Every native of the Forest must have felt the excitement of the season suddenly crystallized on seeing a startled herd race past him for a hundred yards or so, then just as suddenly halt and turn round to gaze in his direction. Alas! this particular excitement has now left the Forest. The deer have vanished. This is sad, because no creature can ever express so perfectly the spirit of an ancient untamed Forest: its beauty, its romance, its pride, and at the same time those immemorial fears that continue to haunt it. To be personal for a moment, I remember how this intimation of wildness came to me one night after an air raid during the Second World War. It was after midnight and I was searching the Forest for evidence of bomb damage. On returning home the verses came to me:

Night in the Forest: the fallow deer
    Shyly out of the mist appear
To brush through bracken, leap and trot,
    Then suddenly halt, as though a shot
Fired by a huntsman riding hard
    Has caught these timid ones off their guard.

Night in the Forest: night of fear,
  By man forgotten, that still the deer
In Madman's Alley* a moment sense
And quivering stand in taut suspense
As the ghosts of the Forest's restless dead
  Transfix their limbs with primal dread.

Shortly before the First World War the number of deer in
the Forest increased rapidly from 169 in 1909 to 239 in 1912.
The highest figure in the annual census is 272 in 1902; but the
mobility of the deer make accurate returns difficult. There
has always been a count on 31 December, but the most
reliable are those made after the first fall of snow. Even with
these there is a danger of deer being counted twice as they
run from one part to another in search of cover or the holly
on which they feed during the winter months.

The late Edward North Buxton (the second) used to say
that about a hundred was the number the Forest could feed
comfortably. He recalled that as far back as 1902, according
to the story he had heard his grandfather tell, when the
number of deer in the Forest totalled 272 fallow and 37 roe,
complaints of damage done to crops in neighbouring fields
had become so serious that the Conservators had been obliged
to make an attempt to reduce the herd. A plan had been
devised to get nets 300 yards long and 12 feet high, and hook
them to trees so that the deer could be driven into them.

The progress of this drive is recounted by Keeper Butt in *A
Keeper's Tale* by Fred Speakman. The main drive was from
Hawkwood to Wake Valley Pond. Other traps, with 150
yards of net, were hung in the Clay Ride and at Theydon
Bois. A Mr Richard Porter of Thames Ditton, an expert in
catching park deer, was called in to assist the Superintendent
and Edward North Buxton in directing the exercise; but they
found the Epping Forest wild fallow very different creatures
from park fallow, and at the end of a whole week only
seventeen had been netted.

After the Second World War the increase in vehicular
traffic on the Epping New Road brought about a rapid
reduction in the size of the herd. During the ten years 1948

* A local name for a walk used by the patients in Dr Allen's hospital for
  the mentally disordered at High Beach.

to 1958 the number fell from 182 to 63, according to the counts for those years; but the 1948 figure looks too high and the 1958 figure too low. It can, however, be said that the herd was reduced by approximately one half during those ten years and that its future was rightly seen to be in jeopardy. The first experiment to provide greater safety along the fast roads in the north was made in 1952, when the verges were cleared and the scrub cut back to give animals and drivers a better view of each other. At first the experiment appeared successful; but when the grass came through along the road-side clearings the deer came out to feed on it and the number of accidents increased. The next step taken by the Con-servators to ensure survival of the species was to net—this time successfully—a buck and several does and remove them to Whipsnade Zoo, where, notwithstanding the security of their new habitat, they have retained their native timidity and nervousness, which is so different from the tolerance of humans shown by the deer in such parks as that at Knole in Kent. The first does went to Whipsnade in February 1955 and two consignments were sent in 1956. At this time the possibility of establishing a sanctuary began to be explored. For many years the increased disturbance found in the Forest had caused the does to seek cover outside its confines when the time came round to drop their fawns. The favourite places were Copped Hall woodland and Woodredon, with Birch Hall, Theydon Bois, as third favourite. Both the second and third favourites were Buxton properties, and Birch Hall had been the home of Gerald Buxton and remained the property of his son, Edward North Buxton, the Verderer most keen on the establishment of a sanctuary. This had to be outside the Forest, because of the restrictions on enclosing any part of Epping Forest. In the event, neither the owners of Copped Hall nor the owner of Woodredon favoured the idea, so Birch Hall was chosen, although its proximity to both Theydon Bois and Loughton made it vulnerable unless it could be surrounded by a strong unclimbable fence.

The decision to establish a sanctuary at Birch Hall as the only effective means of preserving the Forest herd was taken in April 1954, but family interests had to be considered, and it was not until 1957 that arrangements were ready to be finalized. That year the Forest suffered grievous loss by death at what by Buxton standards was the early age of sixty-three, of Edward North Buxton (the second) after thirty-three years as a Verderer. The land was to have come to the Corporation on most generous terms in accordance with the family tradition; but with the large sum of death duties due from Col. Buxton's estate the Treasury were not prepared to allow the provisional arrangements made to be completed and new terms had to be negotiated. These provided for the purchase by the Corporation of eighty acres of farmland for £5,500 and to have the use of thirty-four acres of woodland at a nominal rent of half-a-crown per acre. The Corporation would have the additional expense of fencing in the sanctuary, which they readily accepted. Characteristically, the Buxton family were concerned at the high cost to be incurred by this and remembering Col. Buxton's keen interest in the sanctuary they contributed more than half the cost of the enclosing fence. This was finally completed in the early summer of 1960 with three leaps, which were too high for a dog to leap but not for the deer, who would be free to pass backwards and forwards, although it was always expected that the better grazing provided in the sanctuary and the undisturbed quiet of the woodland would induce them to favour Birch Hall land in preference to the open Forest. No deer were forcibly transferred to the Sanctuary, but on receiving advice that the herd was suffering from the lack of vigorous bucks one was brought back from Whipsnade in 1960 and released in it.

It was some time before the deer resorted to the sanctuary in numbers. In March 1960, Mr George Padfield, who farmed Copped Hall land, complained of herds of up to sixty-eight grazing in his fields; but by 1965 the number in the sanctuary justified closing two of the leaps, and the third, the northern one, was modified by the removal of the inner bank. At the time there were seven does and two bucks in the sanctuary and the future of the herd seemed assured. As deer have a strong homing instinct, and settle most readily where they have been born, arrangements were made for a number of does in fawn to be brought back from Whipsnade. In the event, however, they could not be caught and the Conservators had to be satisfied with the transfer of the one virile buck.

The winter of 1963-4 was a bad one for the deer in Epping Forest. During the three or four weeks of the rutting season eight were killed on Forest roads. In all, fourteen were killed between March 1963 and May 1964. All of them contained gunshot pellets. These had not been immediately fatal; but the bones of some of them were diseased in a way that suggested that this could have been the result of wounds suffered earlier.

By 1972 the herd established in the sanctuary suggested the need for expert advice on their care and maintenance. So Mr Larrett Neale was invited to visit Birch Hall. He approved of what was being done to preserve what he described as "almost a definite sub-species different from any other in the country". When he was there in the early summer of 1972 the number in the sanctuary was forty, which in his opinion was about eight more than the acreage could provide food for during the winter months if the natural regeneration of the woodland was not to suffer. Of the forty counted, seventeen were does, which meant that if the normal 80 per cent fertility rate was applicable, and he didn't see why it shouldn't be, twelve or thirteen fawns would be added to the herd the following year, and perhaps as many as seventeen the following year, which would make winter feeding a necessity for the condition of the herd to be maintained. He further advised reducing the number of bucks. Only 20 to 25 per cent took part in the rut. The others never got a look in, so were of little use. He advised that only the dominant bucks should be kept, because as one virile buck can serve fourteen or fifteen does, the policy should be to have one or two master bucks and two or three runners-up. By cutting out the weaker males the females would become more productive. If winter feed were provided the number that might be supported by the sanctuary would be eighty, or one per acre of farmland. When Mr Neale visited again on 29 November 1972, following the year's crop of fawns, he saw forty-seven deer, of which fourteen were bucks, and expressed the opinion that as this was far too large a proportion of males it was not surprising that there were only eight fawns. The February 1975 count showed that the number had risen to seventy-two, and plans were made for taking off a number of both bucks and does annually. One year later the herd, notwithstanding an increase of approximately twenty, continued to be in good condition.

CHAPTER XIII

EARTHWORKS AND OBJECTS
Of HISTORICAL INTEREST

Ancient earthworks

To THE west of the Forest in prehistoric times a trackway was established linking the Thames Valley to the south with the Fenland Basin to the north-east. In the vicinity of the Forest it followed the valleys of the Lea and Stort and came to be defended by a series of Iron Age camps, of which the most notable to the north of the Forest are those at Wallbury, Little Hallingbury, and Ring Hill, near Saffron Walden. Two others, Loughton Camp and Ambresbury Banks, were constructed along the ridgeway running through the Forest to the south of Epping. They were camps of the kind Caesar mentions as being built in days of tribal warfare for the protection of livestock. From them the cattle would be driven out to graze along the fertile banks of the Lea and the Roding, and it is a thrilling thought that the Ditches Ride through the Forest would first be established by herdsmen driving their cattle between Ambresbury Banks and Debden so many centuries ago.

These are the most important earthworks in the Forest; but minor ones, such as the Mesolithic site at High Beach, of which the London Branch of the British Council of Archaeology has shown awareness, arouse interest from time to time and the Conservators are always ready to grant facilities for work to be done on them so long as the credentials of those undertaking it are approved.

Loughton Camp is an irregular oval enclosure, with ramparts following the contours of the ground on a headland approximately one mile north of Loughton and two miles south-west of Ambresbury Banks. The area enclosed is roughly the same in both. Each is between eleven and twelve acres in extent, but the Loughton ramparts have suffered most from the burrowings of foxes, badgers, rabbits and also from local people digging for sand. Sad to relate, the Conservators themselves have not been innocent of offence. Part of the eastern glacis was cut away to accommodate the Green Ride. There are two entrances at the northern end of the camp, through one of which runs a driftway comparable with the Ditches Ride at Ambresbury. The Loughton Camp driftway runs through the camp to emerge on the south and make its way down the slope into Debden Slade and what was formerly the waste on which the Loughton cottagers turned out their animals. The pottery found during excavations of both camps has been of pre-Roman types not infrequently found in British camps.

The advantages of both camps for purposes of protection are obvious. They are also complementary. Loughton Camp is situated at the southern end of an elevated plateau and commands a view towards the south-east extending across the Thames to the Kentish hills. It has no view to the north or west. Ambresbury is equally well situated as a base for observers posted to give the alarm if enemies approached from the Lea Valley, and alarms could quickly be signalled east by the beacon at Epping.

As the better preserved of the two camps, Ambresbury has attracted more attention from archaeologists. From the point of view of the general public it has had additional attention as the reputed site of the last stand of Boadicea against Suetonius. Although there is no reputable evidence for this, the tradition was strengthened by Morant, the greatest of our Essex historians, giving the authority of his name to it. He tells us that the battle took place "somewhere between Epping and Waltham near which a fine camp remains". The truth is that the burial place of Boadicea is claimed for more than one place in Essex. A local tradition, to which the Waltham Abbey local historian, William Winters, subscribed, has it that the obelisk in the park at Warlies marked the spot where she was killed. If this were so it would indicate that she exposed herself in a peculiarly vulnerable spot and perhaps also that she showed unusual consideration in selecting such a topographically advantageous situation for a memorial to her gallantry. Needless to say, this tradition is equally devoid of supporting evidence. The obelisk, which is about a mile to the north-west of Ambresbury Banks, is a relic of eighteenth-century landscaping by a former owner of the Warlies estate. Apart from the lack of supporting evidence for Ambresbury Banks being the site of that decisive battle, military opinion seems to be that it can never have been a suitable site for any sort of battle. But that, of course, is not to say that Boadicea may not have had her headquarters there at one time. The truth will never be known.

As early as August 1881 Major General Pitt-Rivers, F.R.S., President of the Anthropological Institute, read a paper to the Essex Field Club on Ambresbury Banks. On 5 September he followed this up in an address to the British Association meeting at York by expressing the view that the camp was not Roman work, as had previously been thought, but British. There is no longer any argument about this. The irregularity of its shape is sufficient proof of British origin. But in view of the small amount of pottery found there during the excavations of May that year, when a section twelve feet wide was cut through the west bank, he was not prepared to suggest a precise date. The banks were again excavated in 1926-27 and 1933 by Mr Hazzledine Warren, with similarly inconclusive results.

In 1956 excavations were carried out by a party with four objects in mind: 1. To discover the structure of the enclosing bank and ditch; 2. To locate the original entrance or entrances; 3. To search for evidence of the internal occupation of the camp; and 4. To determine the date of the monument. They found that the bank was formed of material thrown up from the seven to nine foot deep U-shaped ditch. On the question of the original entrances, they first thought that the south-west gap, approached from a ride or causeway with ditched sides, was the original entrance; but excavation showed that this could not have been right, and they concluded that this gap had been made when the site was quarried for gravel. The west gap, opposite the highway, produced evidence of a causeway and two butt ends to the ditch, and this, they thought, was the original entrance. They found little evidence of occupation, which suggested that the camp had served as a place of refuge rather than as a continuously occupied site. The date appeared to be Early Iron Age. Further excavation undertaken in 1958 brought to light stone revetment on both sides of the entrance and uncovered a gateway, consisting of three courses of stonework only just below the surface, in which the post holes for the wooden gates were found. This has been the most important excavation to date. It was organized by the London University extra-mural department, and supervised by Mr John Alexander, staff tutor in archaeology, and Mr Robertson-Mackay, Assistant Inspector of Ancient Monuments, Ministry of Works. Loughton Camp was examined at the same time and dated at approximately 500 B.C.

Modern earthworks

Not all the earthworks in the Forest are ancient. Some were constructed by the Home Guard during the Second World War. In 1940, at the request of the Lord Lieutenant of Essex (Sir Francis Whitmore), Col. Stuart S. Mallinson (later Sir Stuart) held consultations with the Metropolitan Police and the British Legion with a view to organizing the defence of the Epping Forest region by Local Defence Volunteers. The response to an appeal for men was immediate and almost overwhelming. So to ensure a proper standard of training a School of Arms was established in a local cricket club. This is believed to have been the first School of its kind for Home Guard Volunteers, and it attracted many distinguished visitors, including Mr Anthony Eden (later the Earl of Avon) and the G.O.C. for London District, Sir Bertram Sergison Brooke. At the time of the 'Stand Down' Epping Forest was defended by eight battalions, stationed respectively at Loughton, Chigwell, Walthamstow, Woodford, Wadham Lodge, Waltham Abbey, Hillman Street E.8, and Wanstead. During the war period it was estimated that 30,000 members of the Home Guard had passed through the School, and that the average strength at any one time was 10,000.

The first trench dug was near the Wake Arms, and the road from that point to the Robin Hood was mined. At the same time provision was made for manning machine-gun positions across the Forest from Copped Hall to Loughton, which the Commander of the London District considered the vulnerable line. Two highlights in the thrilling story of the Defence of Epping Forest during the war period were the outstandingly successful 'Stuart Exercise', in which 30,000 men took part, and the visit of King George VI on 20 July 1940, when His Majesty took the Salute from 2,000 Local Defence Volunteers in a March Past and Inspection on the Rugby Football Ground at Woodford.

Queen Elizabeth's Hunting Lodge

The most important of the objects of historical interest which the Conservators are required by the Act to protect and preserve is Queen Elizabeth's Hunting Lodge at Chingford, now the Epping Forest Museum. The terms of the Act are: "And whereas there is in the Forest an ancient lodge, known as Queen Elizabeth's Lodge, and Her Majesty has been graciously pleased to signify her assent that the same be vested in the Conservators to be preserved by them."

The Hunting Lodge had already stood for fifteen years when Elizabeth I became Queen. In 1543 Henry VIII signed a warrant to Sir Richard Rich for thirty pounds to be paid to George Maxey, woodward of the Chingford Walk, for work at the "Great Standeinge" and for laying out the King's "new park at Fayremeade". This is both the first reference to the Lodge and the first reference to a hunting enclosure in Epping Forest that has so far come to light. The two are related. It was the park that required the Lodge. In 1543 there was already a lodge, known as the Little Standing, on the High Beach side of Fairmead. There was Pimp Hall, below Friday Hill at Chingford, and Langfords at the foot of what is now Palmerston Road, Buckhurst Hill. Until this new hunting enclosure was planned these were able to meet the needs of even royal hunters who had ridden out from the three starting points of Waltham Abbey on the west, Havering-atte-Bower on the east, or Barking Abbey on the south of the Forest.

To appreciate the significance of the new park, as explained

in the handbook "Queen Elizabeth's Hunting Lodge",* on
which the following pages are based, we need to have in
mind that Waltham Abbey was dissolved in 1540, and that
about the same time Henry acquired the two Chingford
manors, Chingford Earls and Chingford St Paul's, as well as
enclosed land at Gowers and Buckerells, which he brought
from Sir George Monoux. The area of the land already
enclosed has not been clearly defined, but there is documentary evidence that Sir John Gower, A Groom of the Stole to
Henry VII, held 250 acres formerly belonging to the
Buckerell family, and that his daughter married Reynold
Pympe, or Pimp. As land at the Little Standing was already
enclosed, the total area of the royal park was considerable.
Further evidence of the King's intentions at Fairmead are
found in the commission to Maxey to make paddocks near
the Great Standing, and in the appointment of so eminent a
courtier as Sir Richard Rich, afterwards Lord Rich, as
Keeper of the new park and of the old and new lodges.
Independent confirmation of the 1543 dating, made here on
documentary evidence, has come from Mr Cecil Hewett, an
authority on carpentry and timber constructions.

The purpose of the building is indicated in its name. It was
to be a grandstand on which the royal party could assemble
to watch the sport, and for the convenience of the spectators
the spaces between the studs on the two upper floors were left
open above breast height. The failure of local historians hitherto recognize the full importance of the construction of the
Hunting Lodge at this time is due to the subsequent fortunes
of the enclosure. Henry died in 1546, and in 1551 the sickly
Edward VI, who showed little interest in the park, granted
the manors of Chingford Earls and Chingford St Paul's to Sir
Thomas Darcy, who in the following year exchanged them
for other lands. In 1553 Edward, to whom they had reverted,
granted them to the Princess Mary, who had associations
with Copped Hall, and in that year Fairmead was disparked.
In the following year Mary granted the Chingford manors to
Susan Tonge, one of the ladies of her Bedchamber. These
changes in ownership, coming in such rapid succession, explain why the name of Henry's park survives only in the

*Wm. Addison, "Queen Elizabeth's Hunting Lodge, 1977".

names of Fairmead Bottom and Fairmead Thicks, and why
the Lodge is not called King Henry's Hunting Lodge. It was
not until Elizabeth I established herself in Forest lore, and
invested the Lodge with romance by riding up the staircase
on a white palfrey to express her jubilation at the defeat of
the Armada, that it became known as Queen Elizabeth's
Hunting Lodge.

The second reference to the building in official documents
appears in the report of a survey commissioned by Elizabeth
herself in 1589, the year following the Armada visit, when
Robert Wroth, John Hill, Francis Stonard, Francis Stacey and
William Rowe, five Forest officers and lords of Forest
manors, were charged to co-operate with the Queen's Surveyor
in examining and reporting on the condition of the Lodge.
They found that the walls required replastering, the roof
retiling, the outbuildings new floors and windows, and the
fences needed to be replaced. The value of the report is that it
confirms the use to which the upper storeys of the building
were still put by referring to "The second [storey] ... for
convenient standing to view the game, the third serveth
likewise."*

During the Commonwealth most of the deer disappeared
from the Forest and *circa* 1666 the land adjoining it was sold
by the Crown to Sir Thomas Boothby, from whose descendants it was eventually to pass by marriage to the Heathcote
family and descend with the manor. The building, however,
did not pass with the land. In a return made to the Land
Commission in 1788 it is referred to as "a Lodge House
standing in Chingford Manor which is repaired by the
Crown". At this time the lord of the manor enjoyed the
dignity and title of Master Keeper of the Chingford Walk,
but the duties of the office were performed by the Under
Keeper, who occupied the Lodge and was paid by the Crown.
This remained the position when the Corporation of London
purchased the manorial waste in the nineteenth century as we
know from the agreement made on 27 July 1876 between the
Rev. Robert Boothby Heathcote and the Corporation concerning several pieces of land and "the Freehold and In-
heritence of all the old Enclosures around and immediately

*K. Neale, "Queen Elizabeth's Hunting Lodge", 1965.

adjoining Queen Elizabeth Lodge" and "all the Estate and Interest of the Vendor (if any) in Queen Elizabeth Lodge". The building had been occupied as Under Keepers to the Crown and bailiffs to the lord of manor by members of the Watkins family for 120 years when it came into the hands of the Corporation, and the connection was continued by the appointment of the last of the line as a Forest Keeper. When he died between 1882 and 1885 his widow continued to live in the Lodge until 1891, when she accepted £200 from the Corporation for vacant possession and emigrated to South Africa. She was succeeded by Herbert Butt, who with his son Sidney established another fine tradition of service to the Forest.

Little is known about the Lodge between the middle of the seventeenth century and the middle of the nineteenth. It is said to have been used as kennels at the beginning of the period, but this may only mean that dogs were kept in an outbuilding. The ground floor was always divided into compartments, as we can see by examining the interior uprights. A chimney stack appears to have been built soon after Sir Thomas Boothby gained possession, which confirms the use of the building as a dwelling at this time. Some time during the eighteenth century the walls were infilled between the studs and encased in lath and plaster between the floors. The first floor appears to have been brought into use for bedrooms at this time; but the use to which the top floor was put remains in doubt. We know that manor courts were held there, and although Fisher, in his authoritative work *The Forest of Essex,* says that he could find no evidence for either the court of Justice Seat or the Court of Swainmote being held there, it may still be thought probable that the lowest of the three Forest courts, the Forty Day Court, or Court of Attachments, in which the Verderers sat to deal with petty offences would be held there from time to time, although none of the Boothbys or Boothby-Heathcotes was ever a Verderer.

Within a few years of the acquisition of the Hunting Lodge by the Corporation of London, Edward North Buxton felt that merely to preserve the structure was not enough, so on 8 December 1883 he invited a few naturalist friends to his house at Knighton, Woodford, to discuss with them a scheme, drawn up by William Cole, secretary and founder of the Essex Field Club, for the establishment of a local museum of natural history and antiquities in the Lodge. The reasons advanced for the scheme were typical both of the man and of the social thinking of those who had worked so hard to save the Forest from enclosure. It was argued that

> The establishment of the museum would be an educational boon to the many working men and others in East London who take an interest in Natural History pursuits, and the presence of such an institution at Chingford would tend to raise the tone of the visitors to the Forest, and impart a greatly increased meaning and interest to this magnificent recreation ground, which would not fail to be beneficial in many ways.

The scheme was rejected by the Conservators, due, it was said, "to the opposition of a high official of the Corporation", who advised against it except on terms that the Field Club could not be expected to accept. But Edward North Buxton was not the man to accept defeat. Those who worked with him knew his reputation for getting his own way, so the supporters set about raising funds to show that they meant business before submitting a second application to the Corporation in 1894. This fared better. An agreement was reached whereby the Corporation received, and undertook to conserve, a collection of Forest exhibits and permanently to meet the cost of maintaining a museum. On Saturday 2 November 1895, the Hunting Lodge was officially opened to the public by Mr Deputy Halse, the chairman of the Epping Forest Committee, with William Cole, the honorary secretary of the Essex Field Club, as first curator.

The original intention was to confine the exhibits to objects illustrating the natural history and antiquities of the Forest as defined by the 1641 Perambulation. In the middle years of the present century the catchment area for the exhibits was redefined to give a better display of objects connected with the present area of the Forest and its immediate surrounding. Several leading members of the Field Club served as honorary curators until 1960, when Bernard Ward, a former honorary secretary of the Field Club and acting honorary curator of the museum, was appointed a Verderer of the Forest. Largely as the result of his advice, the Conservators were confirmed in the view they were already forming, that the time had come for an expert advisory service to be made available on a full-time basis. For this to be done it was necessary to wind up existing agreements with the Essex Field Club so that the museum could be placed under the general care and direction of the Corporation's own museum staff. The Field Club co-operated generously by donating all exhibits then housed in the museum, and by giving assurances of their continuing interest in expanding the collection.

The building itself continues to be regarded as the most important of the objects of historical interest for which the Conservators assumed responsibility under the Act. Its timber framing conforms with the Crown carpentry of the middle of the sixteenth century and is obviously original. The staircase is of blocks of wood framed into timber strings and newels in accordance with the practice of the 1540s.

A major restoration was made between 1880 and 1882 in preparation for Queen Victoria's arrival at Chingford Station by royal train for the official opening of the Forest at High Beach on 6 May 1882. A new floor was laid in the large room at the top, renamed the Banqueting Room, where previously the floor boards had been 'laid to a fall' to allow rainwater to run off them when the floor was used as a grandstand. By the insertion of odd laths between the joists and the floor boards, the sides were brought up to the level of the centre. A fireplace was inserted with a chimney piece commemorating the official opening of the Forest. The studs to the walls, which had long been encased in lath and plaster, were exposed again; window frames were inserted. At the same time the gables were fitted with decorative barge boards pierced with trefoil openings. Another restoration followed in 1897, when it was found that the exposing of the main timbers brought decay to light. About this time a single-storeyed building was added to the ground floor to allow the museum to expand into the first floor, from which the partitions were removed; but it was not until 1928 that the entire building came into use as the Epping Forest Museum.

It is fitting that since 1894 the nomination meetings for the election of two Verderers for the northern parishes have been held in the Hunting Lodge. As we have seen, this ancient office was retained under the Epping Forest Act 1878 for four local residents to be elected septennially to sit as members of the Epping Forest Committee. Independence was always of the very essence of their main function, which was to maintain a fair balance between the interests of the Crown and the interests of the commoners. When the Crown rights lapsed they were no longer needed; but it was a typically wise move on the part of those who drafted the Epping Forest Act to provide for the title to be continued for four Forest residents who could fairly represent local interests to the Corporation and Corporation interests to the people of the Forest parishes. As the Hunting Lodge is the one building that links the people's forest with the royal forest, it is appropriate that the office that preserves the link should be associated with it.

Coal duty posts

A cast-iron post on the A11 road near Ambresbury Banks, another in Loughton Lane, Theydon Bois, near where the Deer Sanctuary comes down to the road, one on Jack's Hill, one at the Nazeing end of Galley Hill Green, and others on the boundary of the former district of Waltham Abbey, all bearing 1861 dating, mark the points of entry by road into the Metropolitan Police District. They replaced the old coal posts, set up to mark the points at which liability was incurred for a tax on coal brought into the London area, originally imposed to finance the rebuilding of London after the Great Fire of 1666. Later, the money raised from this tax went towards the extinction of the City's Debt. The Coal Duty Acts (beginning in 1831) for regulating the vend and delivery of coals in the City of London, Westminster and parts of the Home Counties were amended by the Act of 1861 to include only those parts of the Home Counties within the boundaries of the Metropolitan Police District. In 1889 the duties were abolished.

Drinking fountains

The Conservators have no responsibilities for the coal duty posts, but they are abjects of historical interest in the Forest.

The same may be said of the water troughs and drinking fountains that were formerly prominent features. The first reference to these in the 'Agenda Books' occurs under the date Saturday 10 June 1893, when four landaus and pairs conveyed members of the Epping Forest Committee to Theydon Bois, to discuss with Mrs Moss the erection of a handsome drinking fountain and water trough on the Green, together with seats both on the Green and along the Epping road in memory of her late husband. This, however, was not the first of the Forest drinking fountains. The Honey Lane fountain had been erected before 1880 by Sir Thomas Fowell Buxton. In 1885 one was erected near the gate to Hawkwood Farm, Chingford, and another near the end of the Spanish Chestnut Avenue at Wanstead. Most of the fountains were the gift of the Metropolitan Drinking Fountain Association, from whom a letter was received in December 1897 seeking permission to erect a granite fountain on Wanstead Flats in memory of Joseph Fry. The idea caught on and several private donors entered the field, notably Sir Edwin Durning Lawrence, Bart., M.P., who in 1899 presented one for erection near Queen Elizabeth's Hunting Lodge. It still stands about eighty yards to the east of the Lodge, behind the former Butler's Retreat. They were all received appreciatively by the Conservators, but it soon became clear that their maintenance would become a problem, so arrangements were made with the respective local authorities for their care, which was not unreasonable since the local authorities were responsible for the supply of the water and equally for its purity.

Several of the cattle troughs have survived, but most of the fountains suffered so badly from vandalism that in 1960 it was decided that any that had become eyesores should be removed. Two at Wanstead Flats were taken away that year. The one at Salway Hill is now on an island site, and for the present appears less likely than others to attract the attention of vandals.

Personal memorials

While the Conservators have always taken seriously their responsibilities under the Act to preserve ancient monuments, they have been reluctant to add to them. If applications to erect monuments on the Forest to distinguished local citizens had been granted, most of its open spaces would have become 'Gardens of Remembrance'. Fortunately the Buxton family, whose own contribution to its preservation might well have been commemorated, consistently opposed such a use of the Forest. So only two exceptions have been made: one for a granite block marking the birthlace of the evangelist Gipsy Smith, to be erected on Walthamstow Forest, the other permitting a bronze statue of Sir Winston Churchill to be erected on Woodford Green. In 1961 a proposal was considered for the erection of a memorial plaque at Baldwins Hill, Loughton, to Sir Jacob Epstein, the sculptor, who did some of his finest work while living there; but this was not allowed. No other memorial stone has been permitted; but in 1965 a giant sequoia tree was presented to the London Borough of Redbridge as a memorial to Sir Winston Churchill and permission was granted for this to be planted in Wanstead Park.

Obelisk

The other monument that may excite curiosity is the Pole Hill Obelisk. This pillar was erected in 1824 under the direction of the Rev. John Pond, Astronomer Royal. It was placed on the Greenwich Meridian at this vantage point to indicate the direction of true north from the transit telescope of the Royal Observatory. The plate on it was provided by the Corporation of London in 1935. The Greenwich Meridian, as changed in 1850 and adopted by International Agreement in 1884 as the line of zero longitude, passes nineteen feet to the east of the pillar.

Other reminders of the past remain in fragments of purlieu bank marking parish boundaries, and in the old drove roads: Epping Long Green, Galley Hill, Green Lane, Blind Lane, Tuttlebee Lane, and one from Bell Common, past Great Gregories farm to Theydon Bois. These were kept open at least since medieval times by cattle driven through the Forest from Scotland and Yorkshire when the main roads were fraught with danger. On emerging, the cattle continued their long journey on foot to the marshes of the Lea and Thames Valleys—notably to the lush pastures of Dagenham and Barking—before going on to Smithfield to be slaughtered.

CHAPTER XIV

THE CONSERVATION CENTRE

IT WAS not until 1971 that the Conservators established their own Field Studies Centre at High Beach, although the Forest had always been a favourite resort for naturalists. Their needs had been fully met by such independent societies as the Essex Field Club, which since its foundation had organized visits and invited distinguished speakers to address meetings on every aspect of its natural history and antiquities. The Club's part in establishing a museum at Queen Elizabeth's Hunting Lodge has already been described; its journal, *The Essex Naturalist*, is a rich mine of Forest lore. But the catering had been for adults only during the early years of Corporation control. It was the increasing interest shown by schoolchildren, many of whom had been evacuated into the country during the Second World War, that led to the establishment of the Conservators' own Field Studies Centre.

It cannot be claimed that this was the first in the field, although it was the first to be purpose-built. The first Centre actually established in the Forest was at Jubilee Retreat, Chingford, where in 1955 Walthamstow Education Committee instituted a Nature Study Centre in premises leased to the Essex County Council in 1947 for use in connection with the sports pitches on Chingford Plain. This lease was renewed in 1952. Then in 1953 the County Council permitted Walthamstow to use the premises for open-air education of handicapped children, and it was from these classes that the Jubilee Retreat Centre developed. It proved so successful that in 1960 a second Centre, again in a building formerly used as a Retreat, was opened. This was at Roserville, renamed Roseville after being purchased by Fred Speakman, the naturalist, who was in charge of the classes there until his retirement in 1969.

The value of the services provided by these Centres prompted the Forest Superintendent to ask whether they should not be made available to a much wider public by the Corporation itself. In a Report to the Epping Forest Committee on the Jubilee Retreat in October 1965 he wrote:

It seems to me desirable that the benefits of a Field Study Centre should be available to others, and accordingly I suggest for your consideration the proposal that the Corporation, as Conservators of Epping Forest, should themselves undertake the construction of a fully equipped Field Centre. As I envisage it, it would be available on appropriate terms to all local Education Authorities for Field Study activities.

At the December meeting following this Report the committee resolved: "That this Committee are in favour in principle of the proposal of the Superintendent that a Field Study Centre should be provided and maintained by the Corporation, and that he be authorised to discuss the matter upon this basis with appropriate authorities, reporting further as may be practicable."

In 1967 the Committee got so far as to decide that the Centre should be at High Beach, and in the following year clarified their ideas about the kind of services they might best provide. It is at this point that references to an Epping Forest Nature Centre disappear from the Committee minutes and references to an Epping Forest Conservation Centre take their place. The explanation of this is that conservation had come to the fore in the public mind as a result of sensational disclosures about the threat to the natural environment of rapidly expanding industries discharging waste, of the pollution of the atmosphere by traffic, and of the rivers by industrial effluent. It was felt that a Centre organized to awaken in children a love of Epping Forest, and to educate the public generally on the importance of conserving open spaces, would appeal to others as well as naturalists. Moreover, it would be a challenge to the Corporation of London itself as the authority charged with the conservation of this unique area, which would be inestimably safer if generations of children passing through the schools of the Forest towns and villages could be trained to appreciate the value of living in a natural environment, and of the precious heritage they had at their doors.

Imbued with this spirit, the Committee resolved to recommend to the Court of Common Council that such a Centre be built; but, while accepting the recommendation in principle, the Corporation wanted to know who would run it and what it would cost. Fortunately, the Superintendent was ready with a practical proposal. He had discussed the project with Professor W. F. Grimes, chairman of the Executive Committee of the Field Studies Council, who had been authorized by his committee to lend whatever support the Council could to examining a proposal for co-operation between the Corporation of London and the Field Studies Council in establishing such a Centre in the Forest. The proposal to be examined was that the centre should be built and equipped by the Corporation and run by the Field Studies Council as the Corporation's agents. But it should be a Centre run on new lines.

From the Corporation's point of view it was important that publicizing the value of the Forest to the public generally should be prominent in its activities. Although the Corporation could still take pride in its long-established role as a pioneer in conservation and its record in the management of open spaces in and around London, it had to be recognized that there were now many other conservationist bodies, notably the National Trust and Countryside Commission, all eager to prove their strength in countering urbanization. Some of these were providing information services which could only be provided officially in Epping Forest by amateurs, albeit well-informed amateurs, apart from the Superintendent himself and the curator at Queen Elizabeth's Hunting Lodge. So it was accepted from the outset that the information service expected from the new Centre would be on a much wider scale than anything provided by existing Centres run by the Field Studies Council, and that the Corporation would bear the cost of this.

The climate of public opinion was favourable for such a project. A growing consciousness of the need for nature conservation was to be found in other countries. There were plans in America for conserving green islands as open spaces for large communities. These were selected areas of uncultivated land, with geological features, flora, fauna, and natural characteristics evolved over centuries that were conveniently located for both recreation and study by town-dwellers. Behind these projects was the same will to awaken in children a love of Nature and a sense of wonder at its infinite variety and beauty. This, it was hoped, would later encourage young people to direct their energies into healthier exploits and enable them to recover a sense of their place in Nature's design for the good life. They would find sources of pleasure that could only be found in a natural environment. Families would be able to recover the joys of spending quiet hours together away from the bustle of town life, and old people would regain the sense of belonging to the established order of life that is so often lost to them when they can no longer hold their own in the pay-packet world.

Epping Forest was seen to be uniquely placed to provide such an amenity for the crowded boroughs of north-east London. It had been used for centuries for the organized studies of townspeople with specialized interests—particularly for the last two or three generations by the Essex Field Club. But a service should be provided for the whole community, and this would come well within the scope of 'recreation' as envisaged by the Epping Forest Act 1878. In fact, the Conservators might well be thought to be falling short of the expectations of the Act if they did not enable people to make fuller use of the Forest by helping them to understand as well as enjoy what it had to offer. Moreover, people could not be expected to safeguard what they did not understand. Too many were already using its roads for no other purpose than to reach London on the one side and the countryside of farm and village on the other when they went out for pleasure. There was also the threat for commercial uses which will be dealt with later.

So plans for a Conservation Centre were steadily evolved without any sense of urgency being widely felt by more than the dedicated few to whom Epping Forest was the centre of their lives until the Duke of Edinburgh, in opening a Wild Life Exhibition at Alexandra Palace, announced that the Council of Europe had nominated 1970 as 'European Conservation Year' and had invited governments and voluntary organizations to start planning for it. The Corporation of London promptly responded to the appeal by deciding to establish the long-projected Centre as its contribution to what was seen as a great and imaginative enterprise. Accordingly, on 16 January 1969 the Court of Common Council voted £70,000, later increased to £95,000, to build a Nature Conservation Centre at High Beach, with a view to "creating a Centre to afford facilities for ecological studies in relation to the Forest".

Questioned about the purpose of the Centre, the Superintendent, Alfred Qvist, who had been the moving spirit throughout, said: "This is primarily an educational project. It is vital that with the increasing use of the Forest, people understand that it has to be preserved and protected. One of the great difficulties is that by sheer weight of numbers people are threatening to destroy the thing they have come to enjoy."

When at the end of protracted but entirely friendly negotiations the Field Studies Council agreed to accept the Corporation's invitation to manage a Centre in Epping Forest, plans went ahead quickly for the establishment of one with three teaching laboratories, one of which would be specially designed for use by schoolchildren, a library and a lecture theatre. The Centre would differ fundamentally from the Council's other centres in that it would be a day centre catering for an age range extending from primary school children to adults. All such novel enterprises depend for their success on getting off to a good start, which in turn must depend on the competence, enterprise and drive of the man in charge. The first warden, Paul Moxey, a geographer, took up his post on New Year's Day 1970. He recognized at once that he had accepted a challenging and responsible job, with an unusually comprehensive range of duties, which was eventually extended to include oversight of the museum housed at Queen Elizabeth's Hunting Lodge. He himself would acknowledge the support he received throughout from the Forest Superintendent, and on the professional side from Professor Grimes, a man with vast experience in such enterprises who proved an ideal guide to pilot the scheme in a manner that would be equally acceptable to both the Field Studies

Council and the City Corporation.

The official opening on 23 June 1971 by Prince William of Gloucester, great-great-grandson of the Queen who had dedicated the Forest to the use of her people within a stone's throw of the Centre, was a memorable occasion. Not only was this the Corporation's contribution to European Conservation Year, it marked for lovers of the Forest the centenary of the lawsuit launched by the Corporation in August 1871 by which this unique open space was saved for the public.

The use of the word 'unique' in relation to Epping Forest is not rhetorical. It has, in fact, several unique features which must increasingly make it a region of special interest to naturalists. As by far the largest area of natural, or semi-natural, woodland penetrating into an area of dense population, yet merging in the north with unspoilt countryside, it is an ideal field for the study of the effect of urban environment on flora and fauna. As it has at no time been managed for profit, or been cleared and replanted, it has had the immense advantage from the naturalist's point of view of control sympathetic to natural processes, with only the minimum of interference necessary to arrest decay and promote natural regeneration. The situation of the main block of woodland on a gravel-capped ridge of heavy clay, deeply entrenched by narrow valleys surviving from the Ice Age, give it a topographical character rarely found near a great city. And so rugged are its contours in the north that whilst its open spaces are crowded with visitors at weekends and bank holidays, the deeper recesses of the woodland are seldom visited except by naturalists and local residents for whom it has an attraction unmatched elsewhere. Consequently its woods, its clearings, rides, ponds and streams yield a variety of wild life that make it an area for comparative studies unparalleled in any other part of the country.

CHAPTER XV

PRESENT AND FUTURE PROBLEMS

IN THE opening chapters of this book it was explained that the issue before the courts in the 1870s was between the lords of the manors and the commoners of the Forest parishes. It turned on the right claimed by the commoners, which was disputed by the lords of the manors, to graze their cattle throughout the entire area of the Forest from the Hams in the south to Thornwood in the north. The commoners claimed that this right was enjoyed by every single one of them in respect of his holding; the lords of the manors claimed that each individual manor was a separate and un-related entity and that each commoner was entitled to grazing rights only in the manor in which his holding was situated.*

Neither the lordship of a manor nor the status of a com-moner in the 1970s is in any practical sense comparable with what it was in the 1870s, when the environs of Forest were still rural. We have seen how great have been the changes in the attitude of the public towards grazing rights and vested privileges of every kind; but the basic change is even more fundamental. The threat to the Forest in the 1970s comes not from a small number of privileged citizens for purposes of profit, but from planning authorities in the name of Progress. The Affluent Society can only be sustained by Commerce, and Commerce depends upon transport, which to the Conservators means roads. Proposals for road-widening schemes are the more insidious in that they are advanced in the interests, not of private gain, but of public weal. Under the Epping Forest Act 1878 the Conservators cannot permit enclosures or the erection of buildings on the Forest except in the interests of manage-

*See page 47

169

ment or conservation, and they cannot sell off land. But they do have power under the Act "to dedicate roads to the public". When they exercise this right, the highway authority concerned becomes responsible for the maintenance of the road so dedicated, but does not acquire the freehold. This means that if land dedicated for highway should cease to be used for that purpose it would revert to the Forest.

Before the 1950s land dedicated in this way amounted to little more than insignificant grants for straightening or widening existing roads with a view to making them cleaner and safer. For example, in 1955 the Ministry of Transport wrote to the Conservators pointing out that many Forest roads had been widened over the years by vehicles forced into the verges to allow those approaching from the opposite direction to pass. The Conservators were asked to accept this situation and permit the County Council, as the highway authority, to metal these encroachments, subject to compensation being paid for the land absorbed. This was granted on certain conditions, the most important of which was that the carriageways along Class One and Class Two roads did not exceed 24 feet in width, that Class Three roads were restricted to 20-foot carriageways, and non-classified roads to 18-foot carriageways, all classes to have 2-foot verges on either side. Compensation was to be in exchange-land, with a proviso added later that where suitable land for exchange was not available a financial settlement should be negotiated. When the schedule for widening on these terms had been prepared, a further condition was agreed restricting the weight to be carried by vehicles using certain of these newly widened roads.

All these matters were discussed at leisure, and it was not until February 1965 that the Comptroller and City Solicitor was instructed to prepare the necessary Deed of Dedication and the Surveyor to proceed with settling the terms of compensation.* Ninety separate lengths of verge had been surveyed and agreed upon, and a further two years was taken up before two additional items in the Theydon Bois district were included. So altogether it took twelve years of protracted negotiations to get slightly less than forty acres of Forest land

*Incidentally, dedication had not been completed ten years later!

acquired for dedication for highway use with suitable compensation, so jealously did the Conservators guard these
precious acres. In fact, since 1878 less than one hundred acres
had been dedicated for highway purposes up to that time, and
it may be claimed that not one of these widenings had affected
the character of the Forest, or interfered with the free passage
of man or beast from one part to another. Little did most
people realize that demands on a very different scale were
already in preparation.

The first of these road-widening demands to provoke wide-
spread consternation affected land at Waterworks Corner.
The Conservators received warning of this in the middle of
the 1950s, and by 1958 it must have been obvious to anyone
using the North Circular Road at the point where it crosses
the Forest, that something must be done if traffic was not to
seize up between Forest Road and Grove Road. Even so, it
was not until 1964 that comprehensive proposals were submitted by the Ministry to cover improvements planned to be
accomplished in stages over a period of fifteen to twenty
years. The most serious aspect of these from the Forest point
of view was that they would reduce the passage from the
grazing and recreational areas of the north to those of the
south; but there appeared to be time for compensation to be
negotiated, and the Corporation found a friendly ally in the
Metropolitan Water Board, which owned adjoining land
then in use as allotments. If this land could be acquired by
the Corporation in compensation for the land to be dedicated,
a new north-south access would be gained on the west side of
the waterworks and mutilation of the Forest at this
vulnerable point would be averted.

While this scheme was being considered by the Conservators, it came to their notice that the Metropolitan Water
Board had prepared plans for a large underground reservoir
to hold twenty million gallons to be constructed on the very
land on which the Conservators had their eye. If the Water
Board went ahead with this scheme the coveted access would
be lost. Fortunately, the Water Board were sympathetic and
submitted that a feasible alternative would be to construct the
reservoir on Forest land and convey the allotment land to the
Conservators in exchange. As the reservoir would be under-

ground, and the surface could be restored on completion, there would ultimately be no loss of use to the Forest. This seemed reasonable, but the difficulty was that the reservoir was held by the Corporation's legal advisers to be a building within the meaning of the Epping Forest Act and therefore could not be permitted. The story of subsequent negotiations is too long to be told here, but as the result of friendly co-operation between the authorities concerned the machinery for compulsory purchase was employed by consent, and at the end of the day the Conservators had good reason to feel that they had acted as faithful trustees, even if the public failed to appreciate the complexity of the problem, and were at times critical of what was being done on their behalf.

Such criticism is by no means resented by the Conservators, however trying it may be at the time, particularly when critics have not taken the trouble to seek the information that would so often have prevented misunderstandings. The Conservators realize that these demonstrations are evidence of the passionate attachment of the people of East London and West Essex to Epping Forest and are grateful for it. What is vitally important to those involved in public relations concerning Epping Forest is that they should realize that this attachment does not arise from this being seen as the largest area of natural woodland penetrating into centres of dense population in England, nor from its being uniquely valuable to naturalists as a tract of natural or semi-natural woodland maintained with only the minimum of interference necessary to arrest decay and promote natural regeneration. It can only be fully understood in relation to the social history of the Forest region and to the events described in the earlier chapters of this book.

The most remarkable expression of this attachment was experienced at the end of the Second World War. During the war years twenty-three acres of Wanstead Flats were requisitioned by the Ministry of Health and Housing for temporary accommodation. At the end of the war West Ham Council asked the Ministry of Town and Country Planning for this area to be permanently used for housing, and to be enlarged to a total of 163 acres. In 1949 East Ham Council tried to obtain nineteen acres of the Flats for schools. The demand for houses at that time was overwhelming. Could it still be claimed that Wanstead Flats, even although the fight to save the Forest started there, was more important as open space than as land on which hundreds of men and women who had given years of their lives to the service of their country could be housed? That was the question. Many lovers of the Forest searched their hearts for the right answer and were unable to find it. They need not have worried. It was the people who needed houses most who said: "Houses, yes! But not on Epping Forest."

It seems strange that roads, with all the noise and pollution they bring, should now be considered more important than houses.

Despite this, however, it is difficult to see how the Conservators could have done more than they did to hold back the tide of traffic that surged through the Forest roads during the 1960s, or to mitigate its effect. What was allowed at Waterworks Corner and Whipps Cross was inevitable; but if any man thought that the eventual acceptance of these roads in the Greater London area indicated acceptance of them throughout the Forest, he was soon to be taught otherwise. The proposals for a motorway crossing the Forest at the sensitive point at which the woodlands merge with Green Belt land to the north roused the fighting spirit of the Forest as nothing had done since the controversies of the first Edward North Buxton's time.

Detailed information about proposals for a north orbital road came before the Epping Forest Committee in July 1970, after rumours had been circulating for many years about an alternative that did not affect the Forest. In 1970 the Conservators learned that five possible routes were being examined. All crossed Forest land, the northernmost cutting through Mill Plain cricket ground, south of Bell Common, Epping. The proposals did not take the Conservators by surprise because as early as 1967, when the route of the M11 was being examined, it became clear that a link road would be planned later, and that an intersection somewhere in the area would be required to bring on to the M11 traffic from the motorways west of the Forest, and to enable vehicles travelling to the Dartford Tunnel to cross. The shock came on learning that this link road, as it was thought of by most people in those early days, was to be a six-lane motorway.

During the 1967 discussions it was made plain that the strongest representations would be made to get this north orbital road routed to the north of the Forest, and this attitude was reaffirmed in 1970. Subsequent discussions, however, led the Conservators to doubt whether this would be achieved, so while remaining firm in their resolve to protect the Forest, prudence required them to be ready with a second line of defence if the first could not be held. At no time did they forget their obligations under the Act to "prevent, resist, and abate all future inclosures, encroachments, and building, and all attempts to inclose, encroach, or build on any part thereof, for any purpose inconsistent with the objects of this Act". But as realists they could not be blind to the need for a road to take heavy traffic off the already congested streets of north-east London and the lanes of Hertfordshire and Essex. So when pressed they felt it their duty to inform the Department of the Environment that while objecting to all five routes, they were clear that the least objectionable was the one crossing Bell Common. Their resistance to the others would be total, but if after full enquiry it were found impracticable to bypass the Forest entirely, they would be willing to discuss further this northernmost crossing provided it could be tunnelled through the Forest ridge.

The Verderers, who are elected by the commoners of the Forest parishes, were vulnerable to attack at this time as the result of the Corporation's decision to take all necessary action to defend the Forest on their own behalf without involving themselves with any local organizations. Local people understandably felt that as they were fighting for the Forest they should be able to look to the Conservators for advice and support. No one was more vulnerable to this criticism than I was. At the time I happened to be president of more than one local organization, and in particular of the Upshire Preservation Society, which was the most vocal and enterprising in this 'Save Epping Forest' movement. In fact, I was never embarrassed, although I had to take quite a few knocks. The role of the Verderers while they were judicial officers under the Crown was to represent honestly and fearlessly the

Crown's rights to the commoners and the commoners' rights to the Crown. In the twentieth century it was merely necessary to substitute 'Corporation of London' for 'Crown', and there was never any risk of being disloyal to either, because I was so firmly convinced that the Corporation's detachment from the interests of neighbouring communities, which during the early stages of the controversy were frequently diametrically opposed to each other, was vital. The Epping Forest Committee had been expanded into the Epping Forest and Open Spaces Committee, with responsibility for all the Corporation's open spaces. There had been a not dissimilar conflict over proposals to run a road through Burnham Beeches. In that contest the Corporation achieved complete success in warding off the threat, which it could not have done if it had become involved in conflicting local interests. It should, however, be stated that although local organizations in the Epping Forest district in the early days tended to be intent on saving their own cabbage patches by pushing the road through their neighbour's they did finally unite on the broad front of the Forest and the Green Belt. Nevertheless, as the sole responsibility of the Conservators was in relation to the rights of the public at large in Epping Forest, and the maintenance of its natural aspect, it appeared to them indisputable that it would be wrong for them to associate themselves with sectional and for the most part private interests, however worthy those might be.

The Corporation, therefore, stated its attitude publicly in December 1973 in these terms:

When the Conservators first realised that the Department intended this ring road to cross some part of Epping Forest from west to east, they made strong representations urging the Department to reconsider the matter by planning a route to go further north to avoid the Forest. The Department subsequently notified the Conservators that no such route was practicable. In these circumstances, the Conservators acknowledge that the route as published is the one that will do the least damage to Forest amenities.

The Conservators note that the Department are still considering the nature of the crossing of the Forest at Mill Plain, near Bell Common, and that the Department will make a later announcement on this aspect after further consideration as to costs. The Conservators are urging the Department in the strongest possible terms to provide a tunnel, preferably one that is bored, but at least one constructed by the 'cut-and-cover' method. In the view of the Conservators, this is the minimum requirement for safeguarding the Forest environment so far as is practicable in the face of road developments. If this is not done, the Conservators will lodge an objection at the appropriate time.

The Conservators also feel that there is an urgent need for a decrease in the volume of traffic at the present time using the A11 through the heart of the Forest, and are continuing to take advice on whether this is likely to be achieved as a result of the current proposal. Unless it is clearly established that there will be such a reduction in traffic in the Forest, the Conservators will object to the proposed interchange with the A11.

Although the Conservators realise that there are conflicting public priorities in this case, their paramount duty is to protect the Forest for the benefit of the public, which has been their obligation since 1878 when Parliament placed the management of its 6,000 acres in their hands. They wish to assure members of the public that they will take all steps necessary for the fulfilment of this obligation.

It is also necessary to make it clear that when the Conservators refer to Epping Forest, they are referring not only to the woodland and open spaces in the main body of the land they hold in trust for recreation and enjoyment; they are referring equally to such places at Copped Hall Green and the threatened verges at Wood Green Road; but while alternative routes are being considered it would be wrong for the Conservators to make value judgements on the relative importance of the various villages involved.

The threat of roads must remain the major anxiety of the Conservators for many years to come. Eventually we must hope that a more intelligent way of organizing heavy transport will be introduced, making greater use of rail and water communications.

At present, most of the other problems come under the heading of 'Effects of Urbanization'. Most visitors come by car now, and they come in such numbers that they threaten the enjoyment of those who seek the peace and quiet traditionally associated with its glades and thickets. It is well to remember that when the public were given access to the Forest recreation and enjoyment under the Epping Forest Act 1878 the motor car had not arrived. No one could argue that motor cars improve the Forest scene; but they have to be contained, and the most obvious solution would be the provision of sufficient car parks. These are now provided on National Trust properties and in Countryside Parks. In some parts of the country the character of the soil and the shortness of the holiday season make the problem of accommodation simple. This is not so in Epping Forest, to which the public resort all the year round and in which so much of the soil is heavy clay. Two or three wet days make many of the most popular places unusable.

Various methods have been tried. Two of the most successful have been: 1. Reinforcing the surface with specially designed concrete blocks that permit growth of grass between the 'teeth', and 2. Laying plastic mesh.

The main difficulty about providing car parks is a legal one. It is related to the question of public right of access to common land, which is especially strong in Epping Forest because this was the first common to which the public were given the right specifically for purposes of recreation. The question has not been tested in the courts in relation to Epping Forest; but in the case of A.G. v. Southampton Corporation 1969 Chancery Division (unreported), in which Southampton Corporation sought to construct a car park on Southampton Common without obtaining the Secretary of State's consent, it was contended on behalf of the Corporation that a car park was no impediment to access. At the end of the case Mr Justice Foster in ruling against the Corporation said: "It is true that if you consider car parks without any cars parked upon them a person can exercise upon them; but when the car parks have cars upon them, it seems to me inevitable that the space so occupied cannot be used for exercise or for air. In my judgment, therefore, the proposed works will be unlawful unless the Minister's consent is obtained." It might similarly be held that car parks impeded access to grazing by commoners' cattle. It is therefore clear that car parks cannot lawfully be constructed on a common without the Secretary of State's consent being obtained and the Law provides that that consent must be withheld if there is no "benefit to the neighbourhood". In Epping Forest, however, it might reasonably be held that benefit would accrue both to the general public and to the commoners on the ground that the provision of car parks would restrict the damage to confined areas.

Meanwhile the conservation of the natural aspect continues, and with the passing of the years the policy of minimal interference, which is now so rare in the management of large estates, adds to the sum of knowledge of Nature's ways, especially with regard to natural regeneration. We have learnt, for example, the value of birch in stimula-ting new growth. A birch tree grows slowly during the first half of its life, then pushes its branches upwards towards the light, allowing beech and hornbeam to make progress. With-out the cover of birch, beech and hornbeam saplings make slow progress. They tend to develop flat tops and remain stunted. It is not uncommon to find saplings of the same age near each other, the one group fully exposed, the other enjoying birch protection, with the result that the one may be three feet tall, the other six feet.

The hornbeam is the characteristic tree of the Forest, and patches of lopped hornbeams have been left as museums of the Forest as it was before lopping was abolished. Birches tended to invade the clearings after the fires that were so frequent in the early days of Corporation management. As they have a life span of approximately 100 years, many are now in a state of advanced decay. Beeches live for approximately 250 years according to the textbooks, which again provokes the question why so many in Epping Forest have varied from the norm by retaining health to what is known to be a much greater age. It doesn't seem unreasonable to suggest that the former pollarding may have extended their life span.

Beeches in the Home Counties are an interesting study. Those in the Chiltern beech woods are cut down and sold to furniture makers before reaching maturity, with the result that regeneration is from weak stocks. Some of the trees in Burnham Beeches, by contrast, are like very old people who have survived long past their term of useful life. These, at all events, are one Verderer's observations; but in making them I am well aware that, although I believe they are supported by sound evidence, later observations may confound them, and I have never claimed to be more than a very amateur naturalist. In any case, Verderers. unlike doctors, do not have the advantage of burying their mistakes and ensuring that they cannot give evidence against them!

I admit bias; but I believe that consciously or unconsciously most of those who have come under the spell of Epping Forest must have sensed something unique to its character, which to me is attributable in the main to its history. Few may realize that when they are walking through the Forest today they are making their way through the same wilderness of grove and thicket that Harold saw when he built his church at Waltham nearly a thousand years ago; that the rides they follow were first trodden by pilgrims wending their way to the miraculous cross at Waltham, and were later trodden by the monks of the abbey in that same town who came out to serve the various chapels of ease that sprang up in the clearings when the parish system was established; or that it was the fact that the rights of the commoners, on which the great lawsuit turned, predated the division of the area into manors and parishes that gave them the Freedom of the Forest. All in all, we may claim that there is no open space in England of comparable importance in the nation's social history.

It cannot be said too often that Epping Forest is not an open space purchased by a local authority for use as a public park of playground. If it were, it could be replaced by another open space. It is an ancient English forest with a character of its own so strong that for a thousand years it has dominated its environs and cast its spell on those who have come to know it. Everything about its management and conservation has to be seen in relation to its history, and in particular to the history of East London, before it can be properly understood and appreciated.

APPENDIX I

Additions to the Forest and its environs since 1878

Locality	Year Acquired	Acres
Epping	1902	7
	1912	1
	1956	2
Theydon Bois	1889	15
Debden	1928-9	16
High Beach	1920	15
	1950	1
		5.75
Loughton	1944	11
	1963	2.5
	1968	14
Sewardstonebury	1899-90	43
	1964	3.5
Chingford	1930	18
	1941	18
	1956	4
Woodford	1930	38
Highams Park	1891	31
	1928	7.5
Walthamstow	1902	1.5
	1969	15.25
		268.20

Not added to Epping Forest

Locality	Use	Year Acquired	Acres
Theydon Bois	Deer	1961	80
	Sanctuary	1961	34 (leased)
		1968	42
Debden	Under con- sideration	1969	31
Loughton ('Warren Hill')	Under con- sideration	1974	10.25
			197.25

APPENDIX II

VERDERERS since 1878

(A list of Verderers from 1250 to 1878 appears in *The Forest of Essex*
by W. R. Fisher)

Sir Thomas Fowell Buxton	1878/1895	1901/1908	24
Sir Antonio Brady	1878/1882		4
Thomas Charles Baring	1878/1880		2
Edward North Buxton (I)	1880/1924		44
Andrew Johnston	1878/1887		9
David John Morgan	1882/1888		6
Alfred John Frost	1887/1894		7
Peter Gellatly	1888/1908		20
Richard Adam Ellis	1894/1901		7
Ernest James Wythes	1895/1901		6
Ernest Arnold Read	1901/1908		7
Gerald Buxton	1908/1928		20
William Houghton	1908/1917		9
Alfred Savill	1908/1915		7
Arthur Janion Edwards	1915/1929		14
Alfred Kemp	1917/1943		26
Edward North Buxton (II)	1924/1957		33
Lord Stanmore	1928/1950		22
Brig. General Richard Beale Colvin	1929/1936		7
John Whitaker Maitland	1936/1945		9
Edward Bernard Cook	1943/1963		20
Herbert John Chappell	1946/1970		24
Bernard Farmborough Howard	1950/1960		10
William Addison	1957/1966	1967/	
Bernard T. Ward	1960/		
Mark Buxton	1963/1967		4
William Rufus Ide	1966/1972		6
John Edgar Harvey	1970/		
John Garson Romeril Griggs	1972/1976		4
Robert Mitchell	1976/		

APPENDIX III

DEER CENSUS 1882-1974
Count started in 1896

1882   Est. over 100
1883–5   Still mounting

Year	Fallow	Roe	Year	Fallow	Year	Fallow
1896	130	11	1921	119	1949	152
1898	178	35	1922	120	1950	146
1899	177	43	1923	119	1951	173
1900	195	36	1924	84	1952	104
1901	228	41	1925	117	1953	81
1902	272	37	1926	113	1954	58
1903	220	42	1927	110	1955	75
1904	171	36	1928	108	1956	62
1905	138	39	1929	122	1957	92
1906	112	38	1930	105	1958	63
1907	102	35	1931	121	1959	98
1908	126	32	1932	119	1960	78
1909	169	20	1933	102	1961	75
1910	221	12	1934	121	1962	69
1911	209	9	1935	103	1963	65
1912	239	11	1936	102	1964	85
1913	228	11	1937	117	1965	63
1914	142	6	1938	116	1966	45
1915	209	6	1939	109	1967–	No deer
1916	136	6	1940	134	1974	seen in
1917	109	2	1941	132		Forest
1918	129	2	1942	152		
1919	95	2	1943	141		
1920	85	2	1944	186		
			1945	165		
			1947	147		
			1948	182		

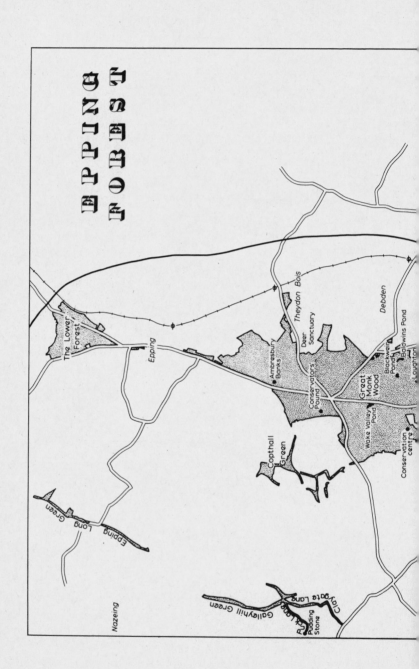

EPPING
FOREST

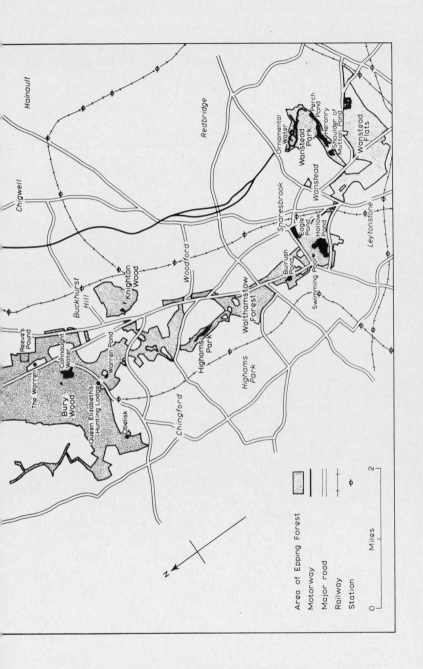

Hainault

Chigwell

Redbridge

Buckhurst Hill

Knighton Wood

Woodford

Snaresbrook

Ornamental Water

Wanstead Park

Perch Pond

Heronry

Wanstead

Shoulder of Mutton Pond

Wanstead Flats

Leytonstone

Reeve's Pound

The Warren

Connaught Water

Warren Pond

Bury Wood

Queen Elizabeth's Hunting Lodge

Obelisk

Chingford

Highams Park

Highams Park

Walthamstow Forest

Bulrush Pond

Eagle Pond

Hollow Pond

Swimming Pool

N

Area of Epping Forest

Motorway

Major road

Railway

Station

0   1   2

Miles

INDEX

187